We Are
Sisters

We Are Sisters

DEE BRESTIN

LIFE JOURNEY®
Bringing Home the Message for Life

COOK COMMUNICATIONS MINISTRIES
Colorado Springs, Colorado • Paris, Ontario
KINGSWAY COMMUNICATIONS LTD
Eastbourne, England

Life Journey® is an imprint of
Cook Communications Ministries, Colorado Springs, CO 80918
Cook Communications, Paris, Ontario
Kingsway Communications, Eastbourne, England

WE ARE SISTERS
© 2006, 1994 by Dee Brestin

Cover Design: Greg Jackson, Thinkpen Design, llc
Cover Photo Credit: 2005 © JupiterImages

Second Printing, 2006
Printed in the United States of America

2 3 4 5 6 7 8 9 10 Printing/Year 10 09 08 07 06

ISBN 0-7814-4315-6

Library of Congress Control Number: 2005938033

To My Biological Sisters:

Sally Brown Frahm
and
Bonnie Brown Rock

You are still my mentors.

CONTENTS

ACKNOWLEDGMENTS

With a heart full of gratitude I acknowledge:

My late husband, Steve: We never dreamed how fleeting our life together would be—but how thankful I am for what we had and the legacy you left to me, our five children, and the world.

My sisters in Christ: You are this book. Loving, laughing, living His love. A special thanks to my perennial friends (season-after-season friends). Thanks also to the following for their stories: Cynthia Clawson, Patti Clawson Berry, Carol Kent, and Jennie Dimkoff.

My biological sisters, Sally Brown Frahm and Bonnie Brown Rock: Mother has just gone to be with Jesus—and with Dad. This makes me doubly thankful for you. In you I still have Mother's love, drama, and graciousness. In you I still have Dad's integrity, enthusiasm, and commitment to family.

My childhood and lifelong friend, Barbara Reeve: For letting me tell our story. For loving me anyhow!

Cartoonist Steve Bjorkman: You are too funny. And you have a good heart, too.

My children: For your faithfulness. For letting me tell our stories.

My team: Christy and Jill.

The Team at Cook: For listening, for believing in me, for using your talents so well.

A Little Help
from My Friends

I have just come from a gathering of women. For three hours this morning the four of us sat in a local restaurant, sharing our needs, our concerns, our unanswered questions—our hearts. Two of us cried after deep confessionals; all of us laughed.... When it was time to go—as other commitments called—we ran outside into the spring rain, light-hearted as children out for recess.

—BRENDA HUNTER

Brenda Hunter, *In the Company of Women* (Sisters, OR: Multnomah, 1994), 19.

CHAPTER 1

A LITTLE HELP
FROM MY FRIENDS

*A*t first moving to Seattle with our two little boys had seemed like a grand adventure. Steve and I felt so amazingly blessed to have found an affordable rental that had a view of Puget Sound. The week before Steve began his medical internship at the Seattle Public Hospital, we sat on our deck watching ferries move out across the bay toward the snow-capped Olympic Mountains, marveling that this was not a vacation spot, but our home! When the tide was out we took our boys down to the beach to explore God's amazing world of tiny sea creatures. We had picnics under fragrant pine trees in Magnolia Park.

But then Steve began that lethal year of internship, a year in which young doctors are often treated without mercy, working every day, every evening, and all night every other night. If Steve had any time at all at home, his consuming desire was for sleep—not family time. He'd mumble a few things while he picked at dinner and then doze on the living-room sofa while his little boys ran Matchbox cars up and down his legs. Steve and I were new Christians but I, in particular, was so immature. I didn't seem to have the strength to face the hurricane winds of that year.

Steve needed a supportive wife, but he didn't find that in me. Overwhelmed with loneliness, weary from caring for the boys alone *(how do you do it, single moms?),* I was focused on my own needs, not my husband's. How I missed my friends in sunny Indiana! Transplanted to this land of damp souls where no one initiated friendship, I became more demanding of Steve, thinking my nagging could somehow make him change our situation. Yet Steve seemed to be sinking lower and lower into the quicksand of an impossible internship and an impossible marriage.

I recall one night when Steve had only been home for one hour before he returned for all-night call, and we spent that precious hour fighting. Or rather, I spent that hour crying and accusing Steve of abandoning us. Steve listened, his face weary, his deep-blue eyes troubled. And then, glancing sadly at me and our two precious boys, he slipped out the door, without a promise of resolution.

I cried most of the night. The next morning I sat by the phone while our sons, oblivious to my distress, played. Three-year-old J. R., clad in a blue Winnie-the-Pooh sleeper and an Indian headdress, pranced around the living room. His younger brother, Johnny, waved his chubby baby arms and enticed his brother into faster and faster circles. Little did our merry sons know that their parents' marriage was in peril.

I stared out at the fog blanketing the Puget Sound. Steve had always been the strong, resourceful one in our marriage. Why hadn't he called?

Finally, at eight in the morning, the phone rang. I'll never forget that conversation—or my husband's emotional state. Haltingly, he began, "I wanted to call you with the promise that things would be better." He paused. "I hoped I could tell you we'd have some time as a family over the holidays." Another long pause. "I just saw the schedule. I'm working on Thanksgiving, Christmas Eve, Christmas, New Year's Eve, and New Year's Day."

Disappointment filled my heart. As I was planning my protest, the sounds of my husband's sobs stopped me. His emotion was so foreign to my ears and it frightened me. Finally he gained enough control to say four words:

"I'm willing to quit."

Quit? I froze, my body rigid, my mouth silenced—but my thoughts raced. *Quit? After four difficult years of medical school? After moving across the country? Did he mean it? Yes, I knew he did! I might say something like that in order to manipulate him, but Steve wouldn't. My dad had helped us through medical school. What would he think? QUIT? How could we? But if we didn't ... could we make it?*

Again, with our situation unresolved, Steve had to go. We were both in tears when we hung up. And as people often do when they feel like cornered rabbits, we each cried out to God for help.

A Little Help from My Friends

J. R. began to fuss because I hadn't let him talk to his daddy, and suddenly I felt propelled into action. I told J. R. we were going to catch a bus, and his face brightened. "Bus!" he repeated excitedly.

A young mothers' Bible study met on Thursday mornings, but I hadn't wanted to go alone. I hadn't had the courage to ask someone to pick me up. Now I dressed the boys hurriedly, stuffed them into their snowsuits, put Johnny in his stroller, and raced with J. R.'s mittened hand in mine to the top of Magnolia Hill. The bus came into sight as we neared the stop, and we waved frantically at the driver. He hopped off and helped me with Johnny's stroller—an act of gallantry and evidence of God's grace. Then we rolled up and down hills until we came to the bottom of Queen Anne Hill, just a block from the church. I deposited the boys in the nursery and climbed the stairs to an hour that changed my life.

I didn't utter one word that morning, but when my turn came for prayer requests, the tears spilled over. I couldn't believe I was crying in front of a group of strangers and I couldn't stop!

A few women came and put their arms around me. A few prayed for me. And afterward, the invitations began to come: for lunch, for coffee, for a walk around Green Lake with our kids.

"Marriage Work"

I've been fascinated by studies showing the impact of women's friendships on the family. What makes these studies particularly intriguing is that they are studies of women who do not necessarily have a personal walk with God. Yet, even for these women, the evidence is overwhelming that women's friendships help, rather than hurt, marriages.

Sociologists have termed this positive impact "marriage work." The reasons for this impact are multiple but, in my opinion, they seem to be rooted in the giftedness that God has uniquely bestowed upon women as the nurturing sex, whether those women are in a personal relationship with Him or not.

When my book *And Then We Were Women* was released in 1994, there was a cross-cultural campaign championing the belief that males and females were essentially the same except for the obvious physical differences. It is somewhat of a relief not to have to swim against that tide as I write this book. Society seems to have acquiesced to the realization that our differences are deep, penetrating to our DNA.

The differences between men and women were evident to me even as a girl. I watched Mother and her friends hugging, confiding, and laughing until tears rolled down their cheeks. It wasn't that way with Dad and his friends. They traded jokes or political opinions, but they didn't CONFIDE, CONSOLE, or CONNECT. They expressed emotion when they sank a deep putt, not when they shared a deep hurt.

Women seem to be able to help their friends in a way that many men envy. This gift for intimacy not only bonds women together as sisters, it often positively impacts their marriages. The reasons given by secular researchers are intriguing.

C. Goodenow, professor at Tufts University, and E. L. Gaier, professor at the University of New York at Buffalo, found that married women who had one or more close, reciprocal friendships were significantly less depressed, more satisfied with their lives, and had higher self-esteem than those who did not have such a friendship.[1] Women like these are more likely to have happy marriages.

A study in the *American Journal of Sociology* by Arlie Hochschild showed that women, when they are empathetic about marital troubles, help their women friends undergo a "frame change,"[2] as illustrated by the following:

Women friends strengthen one another's
marriages by participating in
what researchers call "marriage work."

As women interviewed in these studies recounted such frame changes, their voices carried awe and appreciation for the friends who moved them from anger and negativity to affection and hope.

An extensive study by S. J. Oliker found that women's friendships promote marital stability because they meet intimacy needs that are not met by marriage, and they help diffuse anger and other volatile emotions.[3]

You might think that when a husband and wife have a quarrel the wife's friend would support her grievance and strategize with her friend to help her get her way. One man expressed his fears concerning his wife's close friendships like this: "If Ginny and I have a fight and she runs to see Lori—of course Lori's going to take Ginny's side. She's Ginny's best friend! They're going to run me through the meat grinder!"

But Oliker found that, rather than siding with the wife against the husband, a woman is much more likely to participate in what she calls "marriage work," endeavoring to strengthen her friend's marriage by helping her to see the situation from his perspective, by "framing" the husband in such a way as to "ennoble him," or by diffusing her anger with humor. Here are a few intriguing testimonies Oliker has heard:

> So much of the time I only see my side—I've got blinders on. And June will say, "You know, he's probably feeling real insecure and angry." And for the first time I'll realize there's another human being mixed up in this, instead of just me and my own passions.
>
> Occasionally, my friends will say something about Jeff that puts him in a different light and makes me appreciate him more. He impresses people in certain ways that I forget because I live with it. Like someone will mention something he said that went right past me. And I'll think, "That's kind of nice."
>
> Doreen tells me, "Jesse loves you." And he's this and he's that. She tells me his fine points and puts me in good spirits about him.[4]

This is exactly the kind of help I experienced that volatile year in Seattle from the women friends I met at Bible study. Patti told me how evident it was to her that Steve loved me and the boys. "He keeps his arm around you whenever you're together! And his eyes light up whenever you walk in the room!"

And I thought, *That's true. I am blessed.*

For me, the bond with my women friends went far deeper, for we had the inexhaustible riches of Christ to draw upon. One of the purposes of this book is to encourage you, if you know Jesus, to draw upon those riches in various situations. For as sweet as the sisterhood of women is, it pales in comparison to the power, perspective, and love we have as sisters in Christ.

God has strengthened me by giving me "sisters" who were so filled with Him that the overflow spilled out to me. When I cried upon Lorinda's shoulder about Steve's long hours, she comforted me as any woman might, but she also immediately began to pray. First she prayed for me, but then she prayed for Steve! With compassion, she prayed:

> Oh Lord, have mercy on Steve. He looks so tired, so dis-
> couraged. Sustain him in this wicked internship, protect
> him from so many night calls, protect his health, and
> protect his relationship with Dee.

Suddenly I realized I was not the only one hurting in this marriage. I began to pray for Steve as well, and as I did, God changed my heart from judgment to compassion. Steve came home to a kinder, gentler wife—and I began to see the hope come back to his countenance.

He was smiling again, assuring me that we'd make it. Before I joined the young mothers' Bible study, I felt as if I were swimming the English Channel with two little boys on my back—and we were sinking! But the emotional support I received from my new friends was like a lifeline that not only enabled us to survive, but also to give Steve the understanding and love he so desperately needed in his grueling internship.

More than anything, Steve needed support. If he came home for dinner two hours late, he needed empathy and understanding, not sarcasm or tears. He needed me to do whatever I could to lighten his load—from shoveling the walk to reading Bible stories to the boys. He needed me to abide in Christ so that my perspective and love could keep us both afloat. He wanted a cheerleader, encouraging him and reminding him that this, too, would pass—that the internship lasted only a year, and that there'd be time for sleep and family after June 30.

I was able to become that cheerleader for the last six months of his long-distance run because of the support I was receiving from my sisters in Christ. That was thirty-six years ago, and we never had another year like that.

Steve lost his battle with colon cancer at the age of fifty-nine, going home to be with Jesus. Steve and I were married for thirty-nine years. I am so thankful for the "rescue" that my sisters in Christ performed early in our marriage, and for how blessed Steve and I were for the rest of our days together.

I had a husband who cherished me, who gave me foot rubs every night, who supported my ministry, who prayed over me, and who left a legacy of godliness to his five children, to his medical partners, and to everyone who knew him. I miss Steve with my whole heart, yet how can I be angry? I had so much, and I know it.

How thankful I am my sisters in Christ helped me not to tear down my home with my own hands, as do many foolish women according to Proverbs 14:1. They helped me go higher up and deeper in. They opened my eyes through prayer and Scripture, strengthened my heart through love, and rescued me from throwing away the most precious gift outside of salvation that God gave me.

God gives women a natural drive to nurture. All of the drives God gives us are good, yet every one of them, whether it is for food, sex, or connection, can be perverted. This is when our resources in Christ can keep us from going amok. Let us consider a woman's natural drive to connect.

Driven to Connect

Sociologists tell us that the primary drive for women is connection, whereas the primary drive for men is status. Spiritual maturity tempers these drives in both sexes.

Psychiatrist Jean Baker Miller of Wellesley College's Stone Center explains that the terror for women is isolation. Their sense of worth is grounded in the ability to make and maintain relationships. When women attempt suicide, it is usually because of failures involving lovers, family, or friends.[5] This drive for connection can be extremely beneficial when tempered with maturity, but cruel when it is not.

The easiest way to understand the problems caused by immaturity is by observing little girls. Little girls are territorial and can become treacherous if they feel their best friendship is threatened. I remember Tricia, the little girl who lived next door and looked like Pippi Longstocking, with freckles, red braids, and an infectious grin. Tricia loved it when I told Bible stories and responded to Christ in true repentance when she was only six. She honored me with her trust and often came to me with her joys and sorrows. One day I was getting my newspaper when Tricia came running up to me, braids bouncing, bursting to tell me:

> "Mrs. Brestin, guess what?"
> "What, Tricia?"
> "I have a new friend! Her name is Jill. She's *so* nice. She asked me to sit with her at lunch yesterday, and today I saved her a seat! We walked part way home together and I might get to go to her house for an overnight on Friday!"

I smiled, remembering those days when having a best friend was bliss and not having one was misery.

The very next day Tricia appeared at my door with red eyes, slumped shoulders, and a quivering mouth. She handed me a wadded-up note, explaining haltingly, "Jill's best friend taped this to my locker."

We sat down together on the porch step. I put one arm around Tricia and with the other hand uncrumpled the offending note, spreading it out on my lap. As I read it through, I had to suppress a smile despite my compassion for my wounded little neighbor, not only at the humor in the note but at the delight I felt in having captured a perfect specimen of the treachery of girls.

I shook my head when I realized how completely justified Kelly felt, for these are friendship principles little girls live and die by! I knew this note *had* to go in this book.

> Dear Tricia,
>
> Stay away from Jill. Jill is my best friend and you are trespassing.
>
> - Don't save Jill a seat at lunch.
> - Don't wait for her at her locker.
> - Don't give her notes in the hall.
>
> Is this clear?
>
> Jill is my best friend and you must find a different best friend. Stay away!!!
>
> Love, Kelly

While this demanding possessiveness is characteristic of little girls, we as women, though more subtle, can have similar feelings. Whenever we think anyone or anything can meet our deepest needs, we make that person or that thing an idol. We cling to them too tightly, we demand too much, and we are angry at anyone or anything that threatens our access to that idol.

When I demanded that Steve be able to meet my deepest

needs as a young wife in Seattle, I had the same distorted perspective as Kelly displayed in her note to Tricia.

As women mature, they usually find more than one source with whom to connect—a married woman will connect with her husband and a few good women friends. However, the healthiest change occurs if a woman matures spiritually and learns how to depend on God. She still treasures and nurtures her human relationships, but her dependence shifts toward the One who will never move away, betray her, or die.

Jesus is real—He is as close as your very breath. He longs to be your Protector, Provider, Confidant, and Comforter. In the Narnia books, the children's series by C. S. Lewis, the children keep moving higher up and deeper in.

Though you may know the Lord, you may be camped out in the clefts of the rock, like the Shulamite maiden in Song of Solomon 2:14. She was content to know the Lord, but was afraid to go higher. We all have times when we feel that way, and that's when we are so blessed if we get a little help from our friends, help to go higher up and deeper in.

Higher Up and Deeper In

In *We Are Sisters,* I believe you will reflect on the wonderful strengths God gave you as a woman. I hope you will also be encouraged to consider how to use these strengths under the guidance of the Holy Spirit. Even women who don't know the Lord are blessed by one another's friendship, but *there is so much more.*

I'd like to begin with our bond as females. Though there are exceptions, women generally have a gift that most males do not have. We seem to know, intuitively, how to connect. *Recognizing* this God-given gift is the first step in unwrapping it.

I can't wait to introduce you to Barbara, my very best friend from childhood. Though she has not yet put her trust in Jesus, she certainly has a female's gift for intimacy—a gift that has endeared her to me since we were three years old.

A LITTLE HELP FROM MY FRIENDS

Reflections

Action Points

THE WAY WE WERE

Friendship is a living thing that lasts only as long as it is nourished with kindness, empathy, and understanding.

—Author unknown

CHAPTER 2

THE WAY WE WERE

*W*e were at the lake and Barbara arrived, as she always does, with flamboyance. I was out on the water on a large, anchored wooden raft, teaching my daughters, Sally and Anne, how to do back dives. Barbara's whoops of greeting echoed across the bay.

"HELLOOO! HELLOOO! I AM HAPPEEEE TO BE IN EPHRAIM! YES! YES! IT IS GOOD! HELLOOO MY FAMILY! HELLOOOOOOOOOOOO!!!"

Anne, then eight, whom we'd adopted two years before from an orphanage in Korea, had never met Barbara. Mesmerized, Anne stood up slowly and squinted at the woman hollering on the shore: "Mom, who is that lady?"

Sally and I exchanged knowing smiles.

Enthusiastically, I explained, "Annie, you are about to meet Barbara!" I held up two fingers, pressed tightly together. "She and I were like this growing up!"

I waved both arms heartily to Barbara who waved back and whooped, "OHHHHHH, DEE DEE!"

I dove in, with Sally following. Anne, bundled in a bright orange life preserver, leaped after us. Effie, our Springer spaniel, a flying mass of black-and-white fur, jumped too.

Barbara bounded down the hill, shouting, "MY SISTER DEE DEE, MY SISTER DEE DEE!" She plunged into Green Bay and swam toward us. When we met, she scooped me up, whirled me around, and cried, "YOUR MAID OF HONOR HAS ARRIVED!"

Anne's astonished face caused Barbara to burst into laughter, drop me, and duck under the water. Anne screamed as she found herself rising from the water on Barbara's shoulders. Barbara shouted, "This can only be ANNIE! ANNIE, ANNIE, ANNIE— what a PRECIOUS DARLING you are! And SALLY," she looked unabashedly at Sally's blossoming breasts, "you are becoming a WOMAN!"

Many of the friends Barbara and I have made as adults are surprised by the intimacy of our friendship, for today Barbara and I are a study in contrasts.

Barbara considers herself an "Earth Mother," living in remote areas of Oregon, Wisconsin, and Nepal, moving from place to place as "the spirit" (not the Holy Spirit) leads. She dresses like a hippie from the 1960s, in long flowing dresses and Indian jewelry, her dark hair, now lined with silver, braided to her waist, her feet perennially bare.

For twenty years she traveled around the world with a much younger man named Craig. They planned to stay together as long as they gave each other "good energy." Then one day they surprised us all with a quick trip to the Justice of the Peace to make it legal and, Barbara explains, to "make my papa happy." Barbara practices yoga in her backyard, floats down the Rogue River in an inner tube, and celebrates the summer and winter solstices.

As a child, she enjoyed shocking people and she still does. Watching my children's eyes widen, she grins as she tells them, "I am an INDEPENDENT WOMAN. Civilization could shut down and I WOULD SURVIVE. When I want a fresh chicken dinner, I simply walk out my back door to my squawking and scattering brood. I catch one and give it to Craig, who slits its throat quickly and mercifully with a razor-sharp knife. We throw flowers to the wind in a memorial ceremony. Then I pluck its feathers and bake it until it is tender and golden brown. I feel proud as I eat him!"

Among a myriad of other lifestyle differences, I prefer to buy my chicken in tidy cellophane packages at Piggly Wiggly. Yet I, a conservative Christian and mother of five, have a deep love and appreciation for Barbara.

The Talents God Gives Us

Barbara has some wonderful qualities: She listens to my children, dark eyes dancing with pleasure; she remembers them when she's traveling, sending them postcards or buying them little gifts in India, China, or Guatemala; and she gives them shoulder rubs and foot rubs, causing them to gravitate toward her like a puppy toward his master. She seems like an aunt to them, because of her love.

Christians, including myself, can be guilty of a snobbery that leads them to believe that only Christians can have wonderful qualities. God can work through stones if He chooses! John Stott, when interviewed for *Christianity Today*, said, "Christians are not the only people who have benefited or reformed society. We evangelicals do have a very naive view.... Morality and social conscience are not limited to Christian people."[1]

The book of Romans tells us that God writes His moral law on the hearts of all people, though it is true that it is possible to sear that conscience and be unable to recognize right from wrong.

Barbara definitely has a strong moral law in her heart. I've seen her special appreciation for the childlike beauty of the mentally handicapped and watched her spend much of the last few years of her life ministering to her elderly parents and to other elderly people, including my own ninety-three-year old mother.

My mother is frail and soon to leave this earth. While writing this book, I am holding vigil at Mother's bedside, wanting to give comfort and companionship, wanting to embrace this parting scene, for though the sorrow is deep, it is not wasted sadness.

Barbara stops in daily with flowers picked from her meadow and with tears, for she loves my mother. Her tears minister to us both. Together we stand beside Mother singing softly *Swing Low Sweet Chariot.*

When God knit Barbara together in her mother's womb, He made her female. Deep within her DNA He also gave her the gifts of confiding, consoling, and connecting.

The Way We Were

My children love Barbara, and they continually ask me to tell them stories of when Barbara and I were little girls. The reason my daughters particularly beg for the stories, I am convinced, is that much about the friendships of little girls is unchanging. The way Barbara and I were a half century ago is uncannily like the way little girls are with their friends today. When I tell them stories, my daughters' eyes sparkle with identification.

Reflecting on the way Barbara and I were as children also gives me insight into the nature of adult feminine friendship. Though we become more sophisticated as women and our motives are not as apparent, hidden in the heart of every woman is a little girl who longs to connect.

Barbara and I grew up together, our birthdays nineteen days apart. We cannot remember life without the other. Every summer, we were inseparable. A path running through woods of fragrant cedars linked our parents' Wisconsin lakeside cottages, and countless times daily one of us was on that path in search of the other.

I would usually awaken first, pull on my shorts, and tiptoe barefoot over the rocky path to Barbara's cottage. I'd tap, tap, tap on her bedroom window until her familiar grin would appear through the glass. Then we'd be off to eat breakfast in our secret circle of birch trees: raspberries we'd picked ourselves and Sugar

Crisp, eaten with milk in its own miniature wax-paper-lined box. We'd swim every day, diving for rocks and floating on our backs, soaking up the blue of the sky and the sun on our faces—a contemplative, private, summer joy we never took for granted.

Barbara has always had a deep appreciation for life, and I can remember her saying, as we delighted in our mutual buoyancy, "WE ARE SO HAPPY!" And both of us, having experienced city swimming pools teeming with hurtling bodies, would sigh deeply, clasp hands, and float.

There is a theory of memory that says you remember more things when you were happy than when you were not—and perhaps that's why my memories with Barbara are so plentiful. We shared not only the joy of feminine friendship, but of summer, and of childhood. All summer long, every day, we played. At night, under a ceiling of stars, we'd splash in Green Bay, cavorting like dolphins, relishing the feel of the water gliding over our skin. Then we'd each wrap in a blanket and lie by the crackling fire in my log cabin, sharing our hearts. If we didn't spend the night together, one of us would be up at dawn to awaken the other for another day of summer magic.

The way Barbara and I played is the way my daughters play today. Our games were rarely competitive; they were relational. We blew bubbles in the sun, choreographed water ballets, and made a jewelry store on the beach with an inventory of shells and seagull feathers. We transformed smooth oval pebbles into daisies and ladybugs with bright enamel paint. When we talked, we connected. We affirmed each other's bubbles, ballets, or bright designs and delighted in the joy of connection. We told secrets and drew one another out in conversation. All this was a foreshadowing of what was to come, for as women we are still affirmers and confiders, relishing the joy of connection.

Unlike boys our age, we were not afraid to touch each other. We fixed each other's hair, held hands, gave each other back rubs, and hugged when we were empathizing—which was often!

Just as some of my most cherished childhood memories are connected to Barbara, so are some of my most miserable. When little girls disagree, they know where the other is vulnerable, because they have told each other their secrets. I had told Barbara, for example, that I was jealous of my strikingly pretty older sister, Sally. Sally's birthday was August 16, and mine was August 22—Mother would often have a combined party for us, on the sixteenth, as my birthday fell too close to the starting of school. On one of those celebrations, Barbara was angry with me about something—so she went for the jugular:

> This isn't really your birthday. It's Sally's real birthday.
> Sally is so pretty. Maybe that's why your mom has the
> party on Sally's real birthday.

When Barbara and I exchanged hurtful words, we would then withdraw from one another. Our separations made us miserable! Had we not been isolated in the north woods of Wisconsin, it's likely we would have turned to other friends after one of our fights, and our friendship, like the short-lived friendships of most little girls, might have cooled and died. But we only had each other. We had to reconcile or go it alone—and little girls are not good at going it alone!

Being deprived of our friendship seemed a greater deprivation than going without food or water. The next morning would find one of us giving a familiar tap on a bedroom window in lieu of an apology. Then we'd be off again, relishing the relief of reconciliation.

Because girls and women long for connection, for intimacy, we are likely to find it—but we will also find that intimacy has a Siamese twin of pain. When you are close to someone, you are devastated by transgressions that, if committed by a mere acquaintance, would be a minor blow.

When Barbara and I were children, our unexpected arguments astonished us, like a sudden summer thunderstorm. We didn't understand that the combination of heat and our sinful natures inevitably produces such storms—nor did we have the maturity we needed to respond in such a way as to minimize the damage. And so we threw our friendship rings at each other and stomped off, like the children we were.

And Then We Were Women

Many adults never learn to put aside childish ways. Often women cannot maintain a lifelong friendship. Some sisters squabble until death parts them. It is vital for our own health, and as an example to our children, to learn how to put away childish ways in our friendships and in our relationships with family members.

Barbara and I remained friends through our college years, and she was my maid of honor when I married. We stay in touch by letter and see each other at least every two years, although we live fifteen hundred miles apart.

Barbara and I have surmounted differences in geography, in marital status, and in views of God. The last difference—and I'm sure Barbara would agree—has been the most difficult. Studies show that soul-mate friendships usually fall apart when one has a religious conversion. Barbara and I have had our ups and downs—but God has answered my prayer to keep us friends despite our differences. I don't always behave maturely (though I am getting better), but God gave me the wisdom I prayed for the first time my faith in Christ caused a clash.

When my first child was born, Barbara flew to be at my side, and I asked her to be my son's godmother. Because I was not yet a Christian, it didn't concern me when Barbara promised she would teach J. R. to worship the sun and the moon and the god within him! Asking Barbara to be J. R.'s godmother was like asking her to be my maid of honor—it was a tribute to our friendship.

A year later, however, I received Christ, and Barbara's promise came back to haunt me. More than anything else, I wanted to rear my child to know Jesus. I realized that I had to withdraw my request of Barbara to be the godmother. Would this end our friendship?

Putting myself in Barbara's shoes, I imagined she would feel hurt, maybe even betrayed. Because I feared her reaction, I put off writing the letter to tell her my decision.

One night after I had finished nursing J. R. and put him—sleepy-warm and precious in a soft bunny sleeper—in his crib I stood and watched him. His rump was in the air, his dark hair moist with sweat from the effort of nursing. He smiled as he slept, and his pacifier slipped out of his mouth. I put it gently back, and he sucked contentedly. Sweet, sweet baby.

As he lay there, so innocent and vulnerable, I was overcome with motherly protection. That night I sat down to write the letter I'd been postponing. I knew that my first responsibility was to my baby—but I prayed that God would protect my friendship with Barbara.

I have come to believe since then that often we fail, as Christians, to really be sensitive to our non-Christian friends' feelings. Sometimes our motive is pride rather than a deep concern for their salvation. We speak in haste, and without love, and destroy bridges. I believe that God, in answer to my prayer for my friendship with Barbara, gave me an extra dose of tact. I also believe He prepared Barbara's heart for what was going to be a difficult letter to read.

I wrote and revised late into the night, asking God to help me speak the truth in love. I told Barbara how I had come to trust in Jesus and how I believed His claim of being the only way to God. I told her that I wanted her involved in J. R.'s life, but I knew we would run into conflict if she continued to be J. R.'s godmother. I told her I'd be devastated if this ended our lifelong friendship, and I pleaded with her for understanding. Finally I put the letter aside for a few days, so that I'd have more objectivity when I reread it. When I did, I sensed God's approval—so I mailed it on the wings of a prayer.

God answered my prayer. Barbara was absolutely magnanimous. She was hurt, but she was able to overlook her hurt in love. In fact, she was so totally forgiving that she enabled me to completely erase the whole episode from my memory. I'm not sure when I forgot, I only know that when it came up in conversation this summer, twenty-seven years later, the whole memory took me by surprise.

Barbara and I and J. R., her ex-godson, now muscled and mustached, sat on the beach together. Oblivious to our past, I began chatting insensitively about my experiences as a new godmother, a role I was holding for the first time in my life. My new goddaughter is heir to the Harley-Davidsons, and I began to describe the christening reception that I'd just attended.

"Her parents have an English country home overlooking Lake Michigan in Milwaukee. They had a perfect summer day for their sumptuous garden buffet. Natalie wore a christening gown that has been in the Davidson family for three generations...."

Instead of drawing me out and pressing for details, the way Barbara usually would have done, she was quiet. Then she turned to J. R. and said, "Did you know I was once your godmother?"

My first reaction was, *Could that be? Did I really ask Barbara to be J. R.'s godmother?* (And then blood rushed to my face as the memory, in detail, came back to me.) J. R., who is a very conservative Christian and knows Barbara well, raised his eyebrows in disbelief. Unable to mask the amazement in his voice, he asked, "You were?"

Barbara laughed her generous laugh. "Don't worry—I didn't have a chance to cast my spell on you. Your mother canceled my godmotherhood when you were still in diapers."

I looked at Barbara to see if there was any bitterness in her expression. There was none. I thanked God for a friend who was able to love me even when I hurt her. And I thanked God again for His help—which I had long ago forgotten!

My children know firsthand that unfailing love is possible, even between believer and unbeliever. Solomon says, "Many a man claims to have unfailing love, but a faithful man who can find?" (Proverbs 20:6). I want my children to witness faithfulness so that they will be equipped to be faithful friends themselves.

Still Connected

One morning this past summer, shortly after sunrise, I was having my quiet time when I heard the gentle sound of a canoe hitting the beach and turned to see my barefoot friend climbing out, wearing a sarong from the trip she'd taken to India with Craig. She caught my eyes, her familiar grin brightening her sun-tanned face, saying, "Do you remember, my friend, how we used to get together early in the morning?"

I smiled back. "I remember."

This time, however, Barbara had a mug of coffee in one hand and a cigarette in the other. And we no longer talked as children. We discussed the mysteries of life. I asked her questions about Jesus until she told me she didn't want to talk about "religion" anymore. Tears filled my eyes at the thought that she might not be in heaven with me but may, instead, face the wrath of God without a Savior. I protested that this wasn't "religion" but "a relationship with Jesus Christ."

Barbara cast me a warning look and I was silenced, fearful of pushing her away from the One I wanted her so desperately to know. And I asked God, in silent prayer, to show me the time to speak and the time to be silent. I asked Him to show me if my desire to stay connected to Barbara was overriding His desire for me to speak. For now it seemed, and I prayed I was hearing Him right, that I should be silent.

We walked along the beach together without words, listening to the same sounds we had listened to as children—the breaking of the waves, the cries of the gulls.

Despite the fact that Barbara doesn't embrace my faith in Christ, I love her, and I am grateful to her. Barbara and I also share something that neither of us can ever again share with someone else—childhood. I feel for Barbara a special love that many women, I have discovered, feel for a sibling or a friend with whom they shared a significant part of their childhood. Though they may be vastly different as adults, their childhood memories give them a permanent place in the other's heart.

As I mentioned earlier, my mother is dying. Barbara has been to see her every day, weeping, for she has loved my mother almost as long as I have. This is the beauty of friendships that stretch all the way back to childhood.

When I am reunited with Barbara, I am reminded of the girl in me. When I am with her, I feel younger, more carefree, less reserved.

I also realize that Barbara and I gave each other something else: We sharpened each other's desire and skill in nurturing. It's natural for me, as a mother, to give my children back rubs, to draw them out in conversation, and to empathize with them. In part, it's because of the way my Creator made me; and in part, it's because that's the way Barbara related to me during our formative years.

I also long to have female soul mates and to be a faithful friend to them. In part, that's because some of my warmest and most comforting memories are of my times with Barbara, and I want to repeat them in this season of my life.

Learning to Nurture

I have come to realize, in pondering why little girls are so much closer than little boys, that one critical factor is the relationship little girls have with their mothers. By our very nature we are connected to our sex. We grow in our mother's womb and nurse at her breasts. No wonder it feels so right to be connected to another female! Little boys, on the other hand, do not grow in their father's womb, but are connected to the opposite sex. When they grow up, if they have a best friend, it's usually a woman.

The mother's role is not only helpful in explaining our driving need for connectedness, but also in understanding why some women are so gifted in nurturing. If you had an especially nurturing mother, you had a head start.

This summer, as I was reflecting on the mother's role, I played Scrabble with Barbara's mother. Although I'd always known Jean to be a warm and caring woman, my research caused me to see her with fresh appreciation. I began to realize that Jean was a big reason why Barbara was so nurturing and affirming.

I hosted a "Scrabble and Pie Party" for the neighbors on the shore. Jean and Andrea, a sixteen-year-old friend of my daughter Sally, were at my table. Andrea grew uncomfortable because her score was so much lower than either Jean's or mine. Though we tried to reassure her that it was because we'd had so many more years of Scrabble games, Andrea was unconvinced and gloomy.

The triple word score opened up and Andrea asked, "Is there such a word as quoze? I have a Q and a Z that I have had for the entire game!"

I raised my eyebrows. "Quoze?"

I was about to ask for a definition when Jean caught my eyes and said, smoothly, "Quoze. Hmmm. Could be. I wouldn't challenge it. Would you, Dee?"

I caught on. "I don't think I would."

Quoze went on the board, giving Andrea eighty-one points, and a chance to win. She brightened and began to enjoy the game. Jean and I exchanged secret smiles.

Like Barbara's mother, my own mother has been a very nurturing woman, uncommonly beautiful and as feminine a woman as I've ever known. My earliest memories of her go all the way back to her lifting me from my crib. She'd cradle me against her soft and ample bosom, and brush my baby cheek with her own soft cheek, which always smelled of Pond's Cold Cream. She'd rock me and sing lullabies in her lilting soprano voice. I remember her swaying around the nursery with me, singing, "Hush little baby, don't you cry, Papa's comin' home now by and by ..."

Women who've been blessed with a nurturing mother are likely to have rewarding friendships all of their lives. Daughters who had a cold mother, or a mother who related poorly to friends herself, have a harder climb ahead of them.

Did you know that the proverb "Like mother, like daughter" is from the Bible? (See Ezekiel 16:44.)

THE WAY WE WERE

Reflections

Action Points

NEVER UNDERESTIMATE THE POWER OF A MOTHER

By the time Caroline was a year and a half old ... we had an elaborate lovers' ritual to follow. When she was ready for bed, in double diapers and pajamas, I'd ask her, "Do you want some mama nurse?" She'd nod or say yes and ... literally run to the rocking chair.... Within two minutes total contentment would absorb her and those blue-gray eyes would close. Calling it a lovers' ritual is not an exaggeration: I was her first love, and the depth and completeness of my response to her taught her about the possibilities of love for the rest of her life.

—CONNIE MARSHNER

Connie Marshner, *Can Motherhood Survive? A Christian Looks at Social Parenting* (Brentwood, TN: Wolgemuth and Hyatt, 1990), 31.

CHAPTER 3

NEVER UNDERESTIMATE THE POWER OF A MOTHER

*C*hildren relate differently to their mothers than to their fathers. As evidence, I submit the following two notes that my husband and I found on our bathroom mirror one morning. Anne, eight at the time, had different messages for each of us:

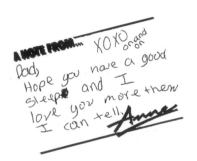

When I asked her why her dad's note had hugs and kisses and mine was about the "throw up in her stoumic," she said, "It's not because I don't love you! It's because you're my mom and I knew you'd take care of me."

However, not all mothers are warm and nurturing.

Mail has come to me in a steady stream since the release of *The Friendships of Women*. As a result of these often heart-wrenching letters, I have come to see how influential our relationship with our mothers is in shaping the way we relate to others, particularly to women, for the rest of our lives. For example, a common response to a cold mother is longing for a woman to love you, sometimes to the precipice of homosexuality, as this letter demonstrates:

> My mother stopped showing me affection when I reached the age of five, telling me I was "too old for that." ... I always wished that I could stay a little girl so that I wouldn't lose her love. Today, as a woman, I have no interest in guys, marriage, or sex—just a desperate yearning to be loved, to be embraced, to be cherished— by an older woman.

Another response to a cold or harsh mother is to pull away from women, to be wary of being hurt again, as this letter shows:

> A few years ago, in an attempt to bring some healing to my relationship with my mother, I opened up to her, telling her how much I needed her. She hasn't spoken to me since. I didn't realize, until I heard you speak at our retreat in Florida, that this is why I mistrust women, don't have any close women friends, and have been promiscuous with men in a crazy attempt to meet my needs for intimacy.

If you had a mother like these, there are some suggested books for you in the endnotes for this chapter.[1] If you have trouble relating to other women, you need counseling to overcome pain for relationships with women, including possibly your mother. Don't be afraid of counseling—and ask the Lord to help you find an excellent Christian counselor.

How blessed you were if you had a loving mother. And how blessed your children will be if you *are a* loving mother. A mother who is nurturing toward her daughter is preparing her for love for the rest of her life.

Carol Kent, the author of *When I Lay My Isaac Down,* is one of the most nurturing women I've ever met. I interviewed Carol when she was giving a retreat at our church. She came to my home after speaking, slipped off her heels, put her feet up, and opened up to me as if she'd known me all her life. Carol's childhood home sounded like a chapter from *Little Women,* with five close and loving sisters. Carol's stories led me to call one of those sisters, Jennie Dimkoff.

Again, I found myself talking to an incredibly warm and nurturing woman. Carol and Jennie are affirmers, confiders, hostesses in conversation—the kind of women you want for best friends. Being with them is like snuggling up to a roaring fire in a ski lodge with a mug of hot chocolate—warmth goes down to the center of your being and you feel renewed, ready to go out and face the cold again. It didn't surprise me to find out that their mother was this kind of woman as well.

Mother Love

Jennie shared with me how, when she and her husband moved from Michigan to Louisiana, she missed her mother and was sometimes haunted by the times she had hurt her mom during her teenage years.

"Feeling homesick, I called Mom and told her how much I missed her—but I never mentioned my other concern. Then one day while we were back in Michigan visiting, I came in the back door, and there she was, asleep in the living-room rocker. I stood there and watched her, my heart so full of love for her.

"I thought of the years she had prayed for and nurtured me, and been there for me as well as for my five siblings. I knelt on the floor and laid my head in her lap. She woke and stroked my hair like I was a little girl again. That day I asked her to forgive me for all the times I had made her cry when I was a teenager. Her response was: 'Oh, Jennie, I love you, and I forgave you so long ago.' Her response to me that day was as nurturing to me as an adult as any tenderness she showed me in my childhood."

Jennie gave me some wonderful insights into the rippling power of a mother's love by sharing with me a talk she gives on Jochebed, the mother of Miriam, Aaron, and Moses. If you grew up in a Bible-preaching church, you probably heard the story of baby Moses in the bulrushes more times than you care to remember—but stay with me, because I have fresh insight for you.

Pharaoh had ordered that all Jewish males be murdered the instant they were delivered. Did Jochebed's hopes soar when she heard that the Hebrew midwives were disobeying the Pharaoh and allowing the baby boys to live? And did they plummet when she was told of Pharaoh's Plan B: to have his troops come in, seek out the baby boys, and throw them in the Nile?

Like many women, I was prone to wild dreams when I was pregnant. Solomon tells us that we dream about what we worry about! (See Ecclesiastes 5:3.) If I had been Jochebed, nightmares of screaming babies, swords, and crocodiles would have kept me tossing and turning.

When Moses was born, Jochebed developed an elaborate plan to save him—and her daughter, Miriam, played a key role. How this drama must have shaped Miriam! If you are an older sister, your mother probably coached you in nurturing your younger siblings, but for Jochebed and Miriam the stakes were life or death. I can picture Miriam hiding with Moses in the closet, honey on her thumb, praying he wouldn't cry when the soldiers prowled past their home.

Miriam probably helped Jochebed coat the papyrus basket with tar and pitch, praying with her mother as they worked. And I'm sure Jochebed role-played with Miriam how to respond if the princess found Moses.

Jennie Dimkoff imagines Jochebed's parting before she leaves Miriam and Moses at the river:

> She holds Moses one last time, feeling the velvet softness
> of his face in her neck, and her heart hurts. She puts him
> in the basket and covers him carefully. She hitches up
> her skirt in her waistband, picks up that basket on her

hip, and steps into the reeds while Miriam, with pounding heart, watches. Then Jochebed comes back on shore and faces a little girl, saying: "Remember everything we practiced honey ... I love you so. Don't be afraid Miriam, God is with you." ... And then she does the hardest thing in her life. She walks away from her two vulnerable children and leaves them in God's hands.[2]

I have little doubt that one of the reasons that Miriam grew up to be the first woman prophet and a leader of literally millions of women was that she had a mother like Jochebed. Jochebed, because she was determined to choose life for Moses, taught Miriam crucial skills in nurturing—skills that would open up possibilities of love to her for the rest of her life.

The Rippling Impact of Choosing Life or Death

One of the reasons abortion rates have soared is that we tend to repeat the sins of our mothers. If a woman who has had an abortion doesn't experience the forgiveness that's possible through Christ, she'll look for another way to ease her guilt. Many become intensely pro-choice, trying to convince themselves and others that what they did was right. Their hearts harden; their nurturing tendencies wither.

If their own daughters become pregnant at a difficult time, they are likely to counsel them to take the child's life. The sins of the mothers, like the sins of the fathers, can be passed on from generation to generation. The proverb "Like mother, like daughter" is actually used in a negative sense in Ezekiel 16:44.

My friend Jean volunteers regularly at a crisis pregnancy center. Repeatedly she has counseled young girls who want to carry their baby to term, but face enormous pressure from parents or a boyfriend to abort the baby.

One morning when Jean and I were walking together, Jean wanted to pray about a sixteen-year-old who had a positive pregnancy test the day before, and wanted to have the baby. The teen was terrified, however, of telling her mother. Jean offered to go with her to talk to her mother, but she said no. Jean later called the girl to see how she was doing, and to see if she needed help.

> When she picked up the phone I could tell she'd been crying. Finally, she said: "Mom is taking me to Kansas City in the morning for an abortion." I asked if I could talk to her mother and she left the phone for a minute. Then she came back, sobbing. "She says there's nothing to talk about."

Ladies' Home Journal asked their readers if they would *encourage* their teenage daughters to have an abortion, and found that 31 percent would.[3] While I believe many of these mothers are well-meaning, I am convinced that the negative impact of pushing your daughter to take her baby's life multiplies in destruction down through the generations.

Women are being lied to, being told this is an easy out—when instead it leads to lifelong pain. When Kathy Troccoli and I were speaking at a women's conference in Wichita, a city known for performing late-term abortions, Kathy had the strong sense that she should sing *A Baby's Prayer*. These are Kathy's lyrics, which she sings so gently:

> *I can hear her talking with a friend*
> *I think it's all about me*
> *Oh how she can't have a baby now*
> *My mommy doesn't see*
> *That I feel her breathe, I know her voice*
> *Her blood, it flows through my heart*
> *God you know my greatest wish is that*
> *We'd never be apart*

But if I should die before I wake
I pray her soul you'll keep
Forgive her Lord, she doesn't know
That you gave life to me.

Do I really have to say good-bye
Don't want this time to be through
Oh please tell her that I love her Lord
And that you love her too

'Cause if I should die before I wake
I pray her soul you'll keep
Forgive her Lord, she doesn't know
That you gave life to me.

On the days when she may think of me
Please comfort her with the truth
That the angels hold me safe and sound
'Cause I'm in heaven with you
I'm in heaven with you.

While the Lord was impressing on Kathy's heart to sing the song at the conference, He was also speaking to the leaders of a local crisis pregnancy center. They called to say that they felt led to have counselors ready for prayer and that money had been given to provide materials to help five hundred victims of post-abortion stress.

The man in charge of the conference was reluctant, not wanting his conference to be "just about abortion." He asked Kathy not to give an altar call about abortion, but allowed her to sing the song. I'll never forget that moment. Before Kathy was even done singing, the women were pouring forward. Even without an invitation, God was compelling women to come forward so that they could receive mercy. Five hundred victims of post-abortion stress came forward, received forgiveness, and went home with materials to help them in their process of healing.

As mothers, not only must we value life, we must teach our daughters to do the same. Lee Ezell tells a captivating story in her book *The Missing Piece* of how she received support when she experienced an unwanted pregnancy. Lee lost her virginity to a rapist when she was a teenager. During that rape she conceived the only child she would ever carry in her womb.

Because Lee feared and loved God, she decided against abortion and visited an adoption agency. The social worker at that agency carried herself "with a military bearing" and thrust a computerized form into Lee's hands so she could help choose her baby's adoptive parents. The form gave Lee a choice of Protestant, Catholic, Jewish, or none. Lee spoke up, asking the social worker to write down that she wanted her baby placed in a Bible-believing home.

The authoritarian woman glared at Lee, and said, "There ain't no box like that, girl. You got your choices. Now don't give me a hard time." When Lee persisted, the social worker slammed her case file shut. "We'll talk about this next time."[4] Then she mumbled under her breath and gave Lee a card for another appointment.

Before she returned, Lee read over the story of Moses and was strengthened by Jochebed's example. Reflectively, Lee writes, "Jochebed did not abandon her child to fate. She did not cave in to Pharaoh's awesome power. She did not let the potential criticism of other women determine her course of action."[5]

When Lee returned to the adoption agency, the social worker stared at her and said, "Now, are you going to give me any problems today?"

With her biggest smile, Lee answered, "Not as long as the line about my child going into a Bible-believing home stays on the application." Lee was neither sarcastic nor militant, which could have been self-defeating. She was, instead, kind and firm, and her request for a Bible-believing home on the application stayed as it was.

Just as God had a plan for Moses, He had a plan for Lee's baby, Julie. Julie grew up in a wonderful home with parents who truly loved the Lord.

And Julie, as an adult—a beautiful young woman who looks almost identical to her mother, Lee—was involved with the pro-life movement even before she knew she'd been conceived through rape.

In the book *What My Parents Did Right*, Julie Makimaa shares how that news impacted her. "I began to speak out against abortion, sharing my convictions—which were now stronger than ever—that every pre-born child deserves the right to live.... I was a prophet called to speak out for the pre-born who had been conceived under circumstances similar to mine."[6]

Lee & Julie

Withdrawal

Experts say that our basic sense of feeling connected or separated from others is rooted in our experience as infants with our mothers. The two most common responses to having a mother who lacks "mother love" are withdrawal and dependency.

Withdrawal is the natural response to pain. In Foster Cline's paper "Understanding and Treating the Severely Disturbed Child" he writes, "It's as if a voice inside their heads is saying, 'I trusted you to be there and to take care of me, and you weren't. It hurts so much that I will not trust anyone, ever. I must control everything—and everybody—to ward off being abandoned again.'"[7]

When we adopted our daughter Anne from an overseas orphanage at the age of five, she was wary and withdrawn. She was raised by a grandmother who had to relinquish her for economic reasons when Anne was five. If Anne had not been held by that grandmother, she probably would have had an attachment disorder, where she would not be able to connect with anyone. (If you adopt a baby or a child, hold her, touch her, stroke her, and look into her eyes!)

Once Anne began living in the orphanage, to her memory, no one cradled her in their arms to ease her pain. Instead, she was perched on a stool and her lovely long hair was shorn. There were hundreds of babies and children, but only a few caretakers with frayed nerves. There wasn't time for stories or hugs! Anne remembers being awakened rudely each morning by a woman who would jostle her and yell, "Get up and help with the babies!"

Anne was not able to tell me about all this for a few months, because she didn't speak English. But I knew the moment I laid eyes on her that she was hurting. It took time and patience to break through Anne's shell, and sometimes I would find myself becoming angry at her lack of response. She became quite ill during her first week with us. When I would pull her on my lap and rock her, she would stiffen. When I would try to coax a smile from her with nursery rhymes or peek-a-boo, she would scowl at me. When I gave her cough syrup, she would spit it back out at me. There were times when I wanted to shake her.

Waiting for Anne to open up and flower seemed to take forever.

A somber little Anne the day she met her new dad at the airport.

Just when my patience was growing the thinnest, God provided a six-year-old to model long-suffering for me.

Sarena Luke had been praying for Anne nightly, for six months—ever since she learned we would be adopting a little girl. I will never forget the day they met face-to-face.

We stopped at Sarena's home, where Sarena ran down the steps eagerly, pigtails flying, to greet Anne. She had a teddy bear, which she placed in Anne's hands.

Anne took that teddy bear and threw it down on the ground.

Resiliently, Sarena reached out for Anne's hand, saying, "Anne, let's go swing." Anne jerked her hand away.

Sarena pled with Anne. "Anne, I just want to be your friend."

Anne didn't understand English, and she scowled at Sarena.

I will never forget Sarena's response. She looked at me and said, "Mrs. Brestin, I don't care how long it takes. I'm going to just keep on being nice to Anne, and one day we're going to be best friends."

God used Sarena, along with others, to restore Anne. Anne discovered that she can trust others. But it took time and the kind of love that doesn't give up, like that of the Lord!

Today Anne is a young woman. For

Anne with boy

four years she was a missionary with YWAM (Youth with a Mission.) This is a picture of Anne with a little boy she worked with in a YWAM after-school program in the inner city.

Some girls, deprived of a caring mother, never have a Christlike friend or a mother figure in their lives. If they don't grow up to be withdrawn, they are likely to go in the opposite direction and cling to their friends with emotional desperation.

Dependence

I've received countless letters in response to the story I told in *The Friendships of Women* of the woman I called Rachel, whom God is continuing to deliver from the bondage of homosexuality. The reasons for falling into homosexuality are varied, but one common contributing factor, according to Dr. Salle deGarmo, who runs a Christian Counseling Center for Women in Denver, is growing up with a withdrawn mother. My friend Rachel also believes there may be a contributing genetic tendency, just as for some alcoholics there is a contributing genetic tendency (though the jury is still out on this).

But Rachel shares, with real hope, "You wouldn't tell an alcoholic who has a contributing genetic tendency, or who has had a dysfunctional childhood, that there is no hope for him! Not at all! We've seen millions delivered through the power of God. It's so unfair to take away their hope, telling them that is the way they are, and must always be.

"So it is with a woman trapped in a lesbian relationship. She will have to make some hard choices, but God can provide a way and bless her with a fulfilling life of healthy relationships. She will have to separate emotionally and physically from the woman she has fallen with, and she will have to get help. She will have to repeatedly offer up her desires to the Lord, BUT SHE CAN BE ASSURED THAT GOD WILL CONTINUE TO DELIVER HER AS SHE ACTS IN OBEDIENCE!

"In time, I was able to have a friendship with the woman I had fallen with—but we had to wait until both of our motives were defined and pure. We are living proof of the power of Christ and so are many, many other women who were once trapped in the bondage of lesbianism. We know we will always be vulnerable to this sin, just as alcoholics consider themselves vulnerable to alcohol, but we also know the victory of continual deliverance!"

Rachel and I have both referred women struggling with homosexuality to Exodus International. Some of the ways they can help are through seminars, counseling, literature, and tapes. They have about seventy agencies in the U.S. and also an overseas network (www.exodus-international.org).

Married women struggling with homosexuality often wish to keep this a secret from their husbands. Knowing how important honesty is in a marriage, I asked Rachel about this dilemma. She said, "If your marriage is not stable, and it is possible to separate from this friendship physically and to draw back emotionally without telling your husband, then you can begin that way. But if you cannot separate or get help without telling him, then you must tell him, or your marriage is doomed anyhow."

Most women who struggle with dependency do not cross the line into physical intimacy, but envelop their friends, driving them away with their neediness.

When we lived in Akron, I met Shannon, whom I liked very much. But before long, I began to crave space. She wanted to see me or talk at length on the phone every day. If I told her what a busy day I was having, or that I needed time with my family, I sensed her pain. I didn't want to hurt her, but I had trouble coping with the demands she made on me as a friend. Proverbs 25:17 says, "Seldom set foot in your neighbor's house—too much of you, and he will hate you."

That was the way I was beginning to feel when I heard the phone or the doorbell. Though I'm not proud to admit this, there were times when I didn't answer, but instead held my breath and didn't move, hoping desperately she would give up and go away. One time when I saw Shannon coming up the walk, I scooped the boys into a closet and hushed them. Five-year-old J. R. said, loudly, "Mommy, isn't this like telling a lie?"

If I had known then what I know now, I think I would have been a wiser friend to Shannon. Shannon was just three when her mother abandoned her and her father, never to return. What Shannon needed, as an adult, was Christian counseling and a friend who would put some boundaries on the friendship. God might have used me to bring healing to Shannon. Instead, I fled—wounding her again.

It is intriguing to me that often God does bring a mother figure into a hurting woman's life and, in so doing, helps her—in Christ—to break the chain.

Breaking the Chain

I found Lee Ezell's story in Gloria Gaither's book *What My Parents Did Right*. When I saw Lee's name in the table of contents, I thought, *I'm not surprised Lee had a nurturing mother—that's why she was able to make the hard choice of life for the daughter conceived by rape*. But when I read Lee's story, it was in a section entitled "Breaking the Cycle." Lee didn't have nurturing parents! Instead, her father was a violent alcoholic and her mother built an impenetrable armor around herself for protection, keeping out not only her husband but, unfortunately, her five children as well. Lee says, "In my home, there was never any expression of caring or love; I knew only defensive survival tactics."[8]

Why was it, then, that Lee was able to become such a loving and nurturing woman? It was because a sister in Christ took the role that her own mother, for whatever reason, failed to take.

Mom Croft reached out to Lee when her own mother cast her out. She saw Lee at church, and with spiritual sensitivity, reached out to her and took her home for lunch. She stood in the gap for Lee's mother, providing physical and emotional shelter.

When we reach out to our sisters who've been deprived of a loving and nurturing mother, we stand in the gap! And by showing them what a mother should be, our influence ripples down to their children and their children's children. And because each of us, as mothers, has weaknesses, we need each other!

I love the comment made by Janice Chaffee, coproducer of the beautiful album *Sisters*. Rhetorically she asks: "Is there a right way to raise children?!"

Then she responds, emphatically, "Yes! Together!"[9]

How true. As sisters in Christ we can encourage, advise, pray, and stand in the gap for one another. To be better equipped to help each other raise our children to be all that God wants them to be, we need to understand them. I will be looking particularly at the world of girls in the next chapter, but mothers of sons will find some hints too. Come with me into the charming, yet treacherous, world of girls.

NEVER UNDERESTIMATE THE POWER OF A MOTHER

Reflections

Action Points

RAISING OUR CHILDREN TOGETHER

"We must join hands—so," said Anne gravely. "It ought to be over running water. We'll just imagine this path is running water. I'll repeat the oath first. 'I solemnly swear to be faithful to my bosom friend, Diana Barry, as long as the sun and moon shall endure.' Now you say it and put my name in."

—L. M. MONTGOMERY

L. M. Montgomery, *Anne of Green Gables* (Toronto: Bantam Books, 1981), 87.

Chapter 4

RAISING OUR CHILDREN TOGETHER

When our family moved to Nebraska, our son John was in his teens. The move was difficult for him and for the first six months he seemed to be without friends. He took a job at the local Ramada Inn and was befriended by some older boys. Then the trouble began. At first the signs were subtle. John was withdrawing from us, losing interest in youth group, and seemed secretive.

One night Steve and I had driven to a nearby city to give a marriage and family seminar. We thought we would be home later than we actually were, and when we returned it was to a house blazing with light and loud music. Thirty teens made a hasty exit, leaving behind empty beer cans.

Steve talked to John for a long time, and John wept. But they were tears of remorse—not repentance. John regretted getting caught. The next night John went to bed at curfew, only to carefully arrange pillows under his blanket, exit through his window, and join his friends.

Here I was—a Christian writer and speaker—but I couldn't control my own son. Pride kept me from telling my friends that we had a prodigal. I tried to fix the situation myself, but John continued his rebellion. I was falling down, but I had no one to lift me up. Not only was I resisting prayer support and good counsel from friends, I was resisting God.

One of the most fascinating seminary courses I have taken was on the book of James. I had often viewed James as sort of a "New Testament Proverbs," a book of wise sayings. But my professor explained that James was not just a book of assorted proverbs, but far more unified.

Though it is true that there are many exhortations, as in Proverbs, for true Christian living—such as keeping a reign on our tongue, caring for widows and orphans, and staying unpolluted from the world—it doesn't end there. It reaches a climax when you begin to feel: *Help! How can I possibly live up to all this?* That is exactly where James wants you, my professor explains, for then he tells you the secret:

> Come near to God and he will come near to you. Wash your hands, you sinners, and purify your hearts, you double-minded. Grieve, mourn and wail. Change your laughter to mourning and your joy to gloom. Humble yourselves before the Lord, and he will lift you up. (James 4:8–10)

This humbling of yourself is the beginning. Then, in chapter 5, James exhorts us to confess our sins to one another that we may be healed! We must take off our masks and stop praying for Aunt Jane's arthritis in prayer group and start praying for our own crippling joints: our selfishness, our gluttony, our judgmental tongues, and our failure to parent well. James tells us that the prayers of a right-eous man are powerful and effective—but how can our friends pray effectively if we don't humbly confess our sins and our great needs?

We Can't Help Each Other
Until We Take Our Masks Off

My great need finally burst the dam of my pride and caused me to take my mask off. I wasn't a successful Christian mother, and now I had *no* idea how to deal with a prodigal. I began to seek out mentors, godly women who had successfully raised children who loved the Lord as adults. I told them the truth and pleaded for their prayers. I particularly remember talking to Shirley and confiding in her: "I'm so angry with John—I can't even talk to him without raising my voice."

Shirley came over, sat next to me, and held me while I wept. Then she said:

> Now is the time to love him, Dee. Rules are important, and you've set those up—but relationship is the bull's-eye. Maybe you shouldn't try to talk to him now—but you can love him. Give him back rubs, play chess with him, don't let him leave the house without a hug. Love can cover a multitude of sins. And John may not repent, for he has a will of his own, but we will pray, and you will love, and we will turn John over to God.

Then she prayed with me and promised to *keep* praying.

I also confided in others, and the praying began. My sister Sally agreed to fast with me that God would find a way to break through to John.

Mourning into Dancing

One night our youth pastor called and asked if we could keep a Nebraska football player who was speaking to the youth group for the night. When I told John that Travis Turner would be staying with us, his eyes lit up. Travis was a star, a hero—and John could hardly believe his good fortune. He was going to get to tell all of his friends that Travis Turner stayed at his house!

Remember when Peter's friends were praying he would be released from prison? He knocked on the door and they simply couldn't believe it was him! That's exactly how I felt the morning after Travis Turner visited. I found out that Travis had stayed up with John until three in the morning, talking to him about his walk with Christ. John came to us, and with tears, said:

> I've sinned against you and against God. I'm going to quit my job because those friends aren't good for me. I'm going to break up with my girlfriend and find a godly girl. I'm going to get involved in youth group and memorize The Sermon on the Mount so that I can live the kind of life Travis Turner lives.

That was twenty years ago, and John has not been a prodigal since. Today he is a godly husband and father of four, training his children to love the Lord.

Research has shown that boys are influenced profoundly by their heroes. Because status is a primary drive for boys, they want to be like the people whom they admire, whom they perceive as having status.

Girls are different. While they are influenced by "heroes" to a degree, research shows they are more profoundly influenced by their best friends. For their primary drive is not for status, but for connection.

Do you remember?

Girls Long for Connection

At our summer cottage in Ephraim, Wisconsin, we spend much time with extended family who vacation in cottages up and down the shore. I remember the summer our daughter Anne met her third cousin, Lani.

Since Anne is adopted, she and Lani are not related by blood, but they decided otherwise. Lani has lovely olive skin, darkened by living year-round in Maui. Her hair is long, straight, and dark, like Anne's. Her coloring was the closest Anne had seen to her own Korean coloring since she moved from Seoul to our racially impoverished land of central Nebraska.

When Anne and Lani met, they stole shy glances at each other, vainly trying to swallow the smiles welling up from deep within—smiles born of the joy of connecting. Within an hour they were whispering, conspiring, and sharing secrets. They spent hours choreographing a dance to Amy Grant's song "Every Heartbeat." When they danced, they held hands, swirled around each other, swayed in synchronization, and beamed at each other, flashing smiles with missing teeth.

As is characteristic of females of every age, they faced each other when they sat. (In contrast, males sit side by side.) One evening I looked out our window to see Anne and Lani seated on the dock. Though the sunset was spectacular, they were not facing it. They were facing each other, sitting Indian style, knees touching. Silhouetted by the sun sinking into Green Bay, their small figures made a triangle, heads touching. They call each other "cousin" and their connection satisfies the relentless hunger females have for intimacy.

The Way Girls Play

The uppermost desire for most girls in their play is connection. Therefore they will abandon a game that is causing conflict. The uppermost desire for boys, in contrast, is to establish status. They often take turns showing off for each other, on their bikes or on playground equipment. Boys are more comfortable with competitive games and less troubled by conflict. Recently I watched Anne and her friend Geri abandon a Monopoly game rather than continue their conflict over when you can buy houses. Connection was more important than winning. They packed it away in good humor and began practicing their cartwheels.

A study of preschoolers by Jacqueline Sachs found that little girls were much more cooperative when they played than were little boys. When they were playing doctor and baby, the boys wanted to take the doctor role 79 percent of the time, and would often get into long arguments about which boy would get this high-status role.

The girls, on the other hand, would ask each other what role they wanted ("Will you be the patient for a few minutes?") or made a joint proposal ("I'll be the nurse and you be the doctor"; "Now we can both be doctors"; "We both can be sick"; or "Okay, and I'll be the doctor for my baby and you be the doctor for your baby").[1]

Amy & Anne wearing shawls

Girls' play is characterized by symmetry. Our home had a bathroom with double sinks. Countless times I peeked in to see Annie bathing a Cabbage Patch doll in one sink while her friend Amy bathed a Cabbage Patch doll in the other. At the same time, they were making plans for continued symmetry. ("When we are done, we will dress them, fix their hair, and take them to backyard Bible club where we will sing.")

Little girls want to dress alike, whereas little boys do not care about this. Little girls will wear matching outfits, fix their hair similarly, or color coordinate. Then they plead to be photographed, and their photographs show the broad smiles born of the joy of connection.

One of my favorite book series when I was a little girl was Sydney Taylor's *All-of-a-Kind-Family*. (Read this series to your young daughters in order to encourage sister love!) In her books, five Jewish sisters show the kind of symmetrical play that is typical of little girls. In the following incident, the sisters have hidden bags of penny candy under their pillows.

> The room was in darkness save for the gas light which shone from the kitchen through the opened bedroom door. Lucky for them! One look at their guilty faces, and Mama would have known that something was up. But Mama suspected nothing.... Tucking in the featherbed, Mama said goodnight to all and went out, shutting the bedroom door behind her.
>
> The fun could begin at last! Charlotte directed because the game was hers.
>
> "First we take a chocolate baby, and we eat only the head." They bit off the heads and chewed away contentedly....[2]

Not only do little girls play differently than little boys, they talk differently.

The Way They Talk

In her book *You Just Don't Understand: Men and Women in Conversation*, sociolinguist Deborah Tannen says, "For girls, talk is the glue that holds relationships together. Boys' relationships are held together primarily by activities.

"When girls are little, one shares a story, and then the other will connect by saying, 'I know,' and then shares her matching story. As girls mature, their matching of experiences forms a more intricate web. They may still connect with, 'I know,' but they are more likely to draw one another out about their thoughts, to affirm, and to empathize. Instead of simply taking turns sharing experiences, they create a stronger bonding experience."[3]

The following is a conversation that I overheard between our daughter Sally and her friend Helen Reeve, when they were in their early twenties:

> SALLY: I'm reading Frank Peretti's *This Present Darkness*.
> HELEN: I read that too! Isn't it great?
> SALLY: It is. But I'm not going to read it at night any-
>   more. I get too scared.
> HELEN: I know. When I tried that, I had to check under
>   the bed!
> SALLY: Did you really? I'm so glad—because I was feeling
>   silly. After I finally stopped reading and turned the
>   light off last right, I heard noises everywhere. I lay
>   there for hours—ready to jump out of my skin.
> HELEN: (laughs and puts her arm comfortingly around
>   Sally) Oh, poor Sally! I understand exactly!

Girls, much more frequently than boys, tie up the phone, write long notes to each other in school, and confide the most intimate of secrets to each other. Girls commiserate much more than boys, because commiserating reaps the reward of connecting. Louisa May Alcott captures this in her opening of *Little Women*:

> "Christmas won't be Christmas without any presents,"
> grumbled Jo, lying on the rug.
>   "It's so dreadful to be poor!" sighed Meg, looking
> down at her old dress.
>   "I don't think it's fair for some girls to have plenty
> of pretty things, and other girls nothing at all," added
> little Amy, with an injured sniff.[4]

Young women are enthralled with romance because romance satisfies their strong drive for connection. They find vicarious pleasure in hearing the details of each other's romances. When teenage boys talk to each other, their conversation reflects instead their drive for status, talking about cars, sports, or topping one another with jokes. Many wouldn't be caught dead admitting to romantic feelings—but would eagerly brag about their sexual conquests (real or imagined).

An example of this occurs in the movie *Grease*, a story about teenagers in the '50s. Danny gives a musical rendition of "locker room" talk. His friends ask him about his summer romance with Sandy and he highly exaggerates their sexual activity in order to impress his friends and establish status. His longing with his friends is not so much for connection, but for status. He also doesn't want to admit that he cares for Sandy romantically because that might mean a loss of status in his friends' eyes. Real men (they think!) stay independent.

The camera then turns to Sandy, where she begins with, "He was really romantic ..." and the girls respond with rapturous smiles of identification. Then we hear the truth about the sexual relationship (it was very innocent—they strolled, held hands, drank lemonade ...)!

Sandy's longing with her friends is not so much to establish status, but to connect. She knows that they will empathize with the joy of romantic connection, and she fills them in on all the dreamy details, and, in so doing, connects with them and provides them with vicarious pleasure.

The Way They Influence

Because the primary drive for boys is status, boys often "hero" worship. The greatest source of influence may be a "hero" rather than a best friend. If your son is an athlete, the Fellowship of Christian Athletes is a wonderful group, for often the leadership is made up of those who excelled in sports and who love the

Lord. A wise mom extends hospitality to godly young men whom her sons admire—because heroes have enormous influence over boys.

One interesting study found that the most reliable indicator of sexual activity in girls was the sexual activity of her best friend. Of course, this can be positive as well as negative. The Song of Songs illustrates this beautifully.

The Shulamite maiden is close to her friends. Repeatedly she warns them, "Daughters of Jerusalem, I charge you ... Do not arouse or awaken love until it so desires" (Song of Songs 2:7; 3:5; 8:4). She is saying in effect, "Sexual passion is so powerful! It's difficult to stop once it's awakened! Therefore, don't arouse it. Don't lift the lid of intimacy even slightly until you are married!" She is thankful that she didn't and encourages her friends to guard their hearts as well.

Your daughters' friends are going to have a tremendous influence on her, yet every mother knows that she can't *make* her daughter be friends with girls who are strong in the Lord. She can make access to those girls easier through choices in churches, schools, and families she invites over—but girls can still resist, for we have no control over their hearts.

It is God who stirs the heart.

The Power of Prayer

Having a prodigal humbled me. When I saw the treacherous rapids of junior high around the corner for our next child, a daughter, I was determined to pray, and to pray with other mothers. I wasn't aware of Moms in Touch at the time, a great organization that may already have moms in your area praying together (www.momsintouch.org).[5] In my case, I asked God to show me with whom I should pray.

One by one, I became aware of different mothers who really had a heart to disciple their fifth-grade daughters. We were from different denominations, different races, and different social classes—but we were sisters, sisters in the Lord. They eagerly accepted my invitation to pray together, and we prayed together for years. I've told this story in detail in the curriculum *Living in Love with Jesus*, but we saw God do amazing things—the girls became friends, helped one another to make godly choices, and were given a plan to reach their public high school for Christ that was amazingly successful.

But just as we saw God at work—we saw Satan on the prowl. One of his favorite strategies is to divide the sheep, for he knows that united we stand, divided we fall.

It began innocently. One day a mother suggested that perhaps we could agree on some standards for our daughters about choices in videos, dating, curfews, etc. If we thought alike, we would have strength in numbers.

The problem was, we *didn't* think alike on these peripheral issues. The discussion was heated before it even got rolling:

> Mother #1: *When are you going to let your daughters start dating?*
> Mother #2: *They shouldn't date before they are sixteen.*
> Mother #3: *Sixteen! They are babies at sixteen. They shouldn't date in high school.*
> Mother #4: *They shouldn't date at all.*

The room became tense, for mothers can be like mother bears when they feel their cubs are in danger. We tried a few other subjects such as schooling and entertainment choices—and the discussion only became more heated. None of us were quick to listen, slow to speak, or slow to become angry. One by one, the mothers left in tears.

The Power of Humility

If we had been wiser, we would have realized we don't have to agree on peripheral issues. Romans 14 is quite clear on this, telling us not to judge our sister on these kinds of choices, but to simply be ready to give an account to God for our own choices. But we were judgmental and prideful.

What is the secret in overcoming the enemy? What is the secret in overcoming fights and quarrels among us? Again, James tells us: "God opposes the proud but gives grace to the humble" (James 4:6). It took me several days to come to the point of humility. But as God was humbling me, He was also working on my sisters. One by one, we confessed our sin, came together, wept, embraced—and saw the enemy run with his tail between his legs.

The Power of the Word

Hebrews 12:13 says: "Make level paths for your feet, so that the lame may not be disabled, but rather healed." Childhood is the time we have to help our children discover level paths. If we don't, they may become permanently disabled in relating to others.

I do not agree with those who feel they should stay out of their children's squabbles with siblings or friends. These are the formative years! This is the time to *train* them to use the powerful tools of Scripture. As mothers, or as mentors, God has called us to this training, to teach the next generation healthy habits that will enhance their relationships their whole lives long. Together we must strengthen one another in the Word so that we can, in turn, help our daughters to walk in truth.

I found that when my daughters are hurting because of friendship pain, they're teachable, like fallow ground ready to receive good seed. When Sally started high school, she also discovered that an older girl from her youth group, whom I'll call Sue, was making Sally a target. Whenever Sally crossed paths with Sue and her friends, Sue would roll her eyes and whisper to her friends. Then they would giggle as Sally continued walking.

Sally and I prayed about it, and the Scripture that came to my mind was, "Do not be overcome by evil, but overcome evil with good" (Romans 12:21). Sally and I role-played different ways she could apply this verse with Sue. Sally pretended to be Sue and showed me how she glared whenever Sally walked past her table in art class. Taking Sally's part, I smiled and said, "Hi, Sue! I saw your tennis scores in the paper. They were great!"

Sally said, "Oh, Mom, I don't know if I can do that. She'll just glare at me." I said, "Probably! But Proverbs 25:15 tells us that 'a gentle tongue can break a bone.' If you are persistently warm and friendly, I think Sue's hardness will break. I'm excited, Sally, to see what God is going to do!"

Sally flew into the house after school the next day and said, "I did it! Sue looked stunned!" And after school I saw her and—you will not believe this, Mom—Sue said, 'Hi!'"

Of course, our plans have not always produced the desired result, and if my child seems to be banging her head against the wall, I suggest that she lay that friendship down for a time and seek other friends. It's important that she leaves the door open and remains friendly, but it's very possible the friendship needs a rest. Sometimes enthusiastic young gardeners can overwater and overwork—and the plants would do better if left alone for a while.

I was impressed at how my friend Connie trained her daughter Andrea in a difficult friendship situation. Andrea's best friend had gotten the lead in a school play and seemed to have little time for Andrea. She had new friends, a new schedule, and Andrea felt left in the dust. Instead of telling Andrea exactly what to do, Connie told her daughter to ask God for wisdom and then to do what He told her to do.

"How will He tell me?" Andrea asked.

"I don't know," Connie said. "He often speaks through the Bible—so it might be when you are reading your Bible, or He might bring a verse to mind—or He might speak to you through a person. I don't know. But He promises that He will give wisdom if we ask. So ask—wait—be alert."

For three days, Andrea asked God. She kept telling Connie: "He's not showing me."

Connie said, confidently, "He will. I don't know when and I don't know how. But He will."

One day Andrea came down to breakfast and said, "He spoke to me."

"How?"

"This morning, I was reading Proverbs 17:17. It says, 'A friend loves at all times.' That's a verse I memorized in Awana—and it was like it was highlighted, underlined, and in bold when I read it this morning."

Connie not only taught Andrea how to respond to her friend, she taught her how to seek God.

The biological (or adopted) sister relationship has parallels to friendship, but additional dynamics are at work. For example, many older sisters can remember exercising their power over a younger sister. Tania Aebi, who is fourteen months older than her sister Nina, reminisced how she and her best friend, "in a fit of adolescent cruelty," tricked Nina. "We gouged out the chocolate chips in some cookies, replaced them carefully with small, black rabbit droppings and offered them to Nina.... Before asking why I was being so uncharacteristically nice, she popped one in her mouth. We then told her what she was eating and doubled over in laughter."[6]

Why is it that big sisters can be so mean and little sisters such brats? How can we overcome the hurts of childhood, put away childish ways, and become true friends?

RAISING OUR CHILDREN TOGETHER

Reflections

Action Points

THE SIBLING BOND

After all this time—you girls still don't realize. Daddy's gone. One day I'll be gone. Children will leave you. So will husbands and lovers. You're the only ones who know each other from cradle to grave.

—Elizabeth Hoffman

CHAPTER 5

THE SIBLING BOND

The sibling bond is unique, and most of us eventually come to appreciate this. We have ties friends cannot have—the same blood runs through our veins, the same mother parented us, and the same childhood homes surrounded us. If you are sisters, your bond is likely to be particularly deep. Research shows the strongest sibling bond (and MCI reports the highest phone bills) is usually between two sisters, followed by sister and brother, and trailed by two brothers.

I cannot count the times a woman has asked me to autograph *The Friendships of Women* to her sister, saying, "She's my best friend!" If there is an emotional distance between biological sisters, it troubles them.

Elizabeth Fishel, author of *Sisters*, found in her interviews a yearning to "unmask and disempower jealousy."[1] If biological or adopted sisters are not close, they long to be. In order for that to happen, patterns of childhood may need to be overcome, or those patterns will be like a barbed-wire fence preventing access into a beautiful garden of friendship.

The Eldest and the Youngest

Firstborns are often serious, responsible, and sometimes patronizing. They are thrust into a role that shapes them! My first grandchild is Emily. Her name means "industrious," which is certainly a helpful quality for a firstborn to have. I remember cradling Emily—tiny and pink, a fragile rosebud—in the hospital room.

I thought, *Here it begins. Here it starts. Poor little Emmie! So much work ahead of you! May the Lord give you strength and wisdom!* And He has. She is twelve at the writing of this book, and I have joked that she has *always* seemed to be twelve. Emily is serious, responsible, and trustworthy. She can keep her sisters and brothers playing happily together for hours, acting as a capable little woman.

She can also be patronizing, even to her grandmother. When she was four I laid down with her as she was going to sleep. Her dad had put stars that glow in the dark in the form of constellations all over her ceiling. Thinking I had a teachable moment, I said, "Emmie, do you know who made the stars?"

She sighed with exasperation. "Grandmother. I know who made the stars outside. But did you know that my dad did these?"

Older sisters work harder, but have also been known to abuse their age advantage. Elizabeth Fishel, author of *Sisters*, explains that "dominating younger siblings gives older siblings an illusion of power in an unfree world."[2]

Parents, as is appropriate, instruct and discipline their children. Therefore, when the second child is born, the first thinks, *Aha! Now is my chance!*

There are challenges for the eldest. Carol Kent, the eldest of six (all girls, except for the youngest), said: "I was the one in charge, but I had absolutely no control. They were naughty children. It was hard work. And I wasn't being paid for it. This is the job of the older sister." Carol remembers the following incident, and I know older sisters everywhere will identify.

Incident remembered by
Carol Kent, the eldest of five
sisters and a brother.

Recording artist Cynthia Clawson admitted to mercilessly dominating her younger sister, Patti. When a third child, "the golden boy," was born, Patti sat on him, and bit him—a lot!

Younger siblings, in retaliation for being dominated, may seek revenge. They pester, they tease, they plot. Occasionally, when my older sisters were undressing, I'd run and hide in the hall closet that housed our laundry chute and crouch on the shelf above, waiting breathlessly for the moment when one of them would unsuspectingly open the door. Then I'd leap out with a blood-curdling yell, stopping her heart and filling my own with temporary glee.

The baby in the family may expect to be the center of attention, to do little work, and to get away with it! If parents don't set boundaries for the baby, the situation is exacerbated.

Sally, Bonnie, & Dee

Recovery Is the Norm

And yet, studies show that most siblings find themselves getting closer as adults. On my fireplace mantle I have a faded black-and-white photograph of my sisters and me as wide-eyed little girls.

We are determined to put away childish ways and relate to each other as peers. Our relationship as sisters may very well be the longest relationship of our lives and we yearn for it to be the best it can be. The older we get, the closer we move together emotionally.

Cynthia Clawson and her sister Patti are soul mates, giving one another strength in their demanding life ministries. Cynthia said, "When something good happens to me, I want to pick up the phone and say, 'Hey, Patti, listen to this!' or when something horrible happens, 'Patti, you are not going to believe what happened to me!' I know she's going to understand. It's kind of like talking to myself."

The saying, "Blood is thicker than water," implies that there is a richness in kin relationships which friends can never attain. Actually, I am convinced that, in Christ, friendships can be as deep as kin relationships. It is true, however, that shared genes, childhoods, bedrooms, and memories can tie you together in bonds that are not easily severed. And parents (and mentors) who help children to appreciate these bonds are laying the groundwork for long-lasting love.

Let us consider some of the bonds for which we can be thankful.

Shared Genes

Sometimes when I laugh, or inflect my voice a certain way, I hear one of my sister's voices echoing back at me. My sisters and I are linked genetically. We have similar voices, a dramatic flair, and flabby thighs.

Sometimes we don't realize how much we are like a sibling until we are with people who know that sibling well. When I visited my sister Sally's Bible study in Austin, her friends kept smiling when I talked. Not because I was humorous, but because my words and facial expressions reminded them so much of the friend they knew so well.

When my sisters and I fought as children, our dad would sit down and give us a complex mathematical theory that siblings shared more blood than any other relation—more, even, than parent and child. Then he would lean back in his chair, smile, and say, "So let's not have any more quarreling among you—for you are sisters."

This is exactly the peacemaking plea Abram used with Lot when their herdsmen were quarreling over land. Abram said, "Let's not have any quarreling between you and me, or between your herdsmen and mine, for we are brothers" (Genesis 13:8). I firmly believe that it is a wise parent who intercedes and encourages siblings to love each other and to become aware of the danger of careless words that can leave lifelong scars. I know how blessed we were to have a dad who continually pointed out the value of the sibling bond.

We also need training when we are young on *how* to get along. Often the most teachable moments are not during a quarrel but during peacetime.

If your children memorize passages dealing with relationship skills, those passages will guide them all of their lives. Our most successful runs at family devotions have been when we've acted out Proverbs. Each parent takes a child or two, plans a proverb skit, and comes back to perform it. Here's a sample skit, based on Proverbs 15:1: "A gentle answer turns away wrath, but a harsh word stirs up anger."

> SCENE 1:
>   SALLY: Who ate all the cookies?
>   ANNE: You should thank me, you're watching your weight.
>   SALLY: [Pushes her] You little brat!
>
> SCENE 2:
>   SALLY: Who ate all the cookies?
>   ANNE: I'm sorry! I should have left you one!
>   SALLY: Oh, it's no big deal. [Hugs her]

We have a responsibility to train our children, not only to promote family harmony, but also to prepare them for relationships for the rest of their lives. A sister is often the first roommate in life—but she won't be the last. Habits learned with a sister affect all future roommates!

Shared Bedrooms

Shared bedrooms are a source of joy and pain, but always of memories. Patti Clawson Berry says that she and her sister Cynthia had a blast. "Cynthia was a very imaginative storyteller, and we'd be under the covers with a flashlight. We had a tiny tape recorder and we'd make tapes until two in the morning." As adults, Patti and Cynthia still share a hotel bedroom when they are on tour. Cynthia said, "And sometimes, when we were a lit-tle younger, we'd come back to the room with pent-up energy and jump on the bed!"

Shared bedrooms are also a source of strife. Cynthia and Patti fought over the invisible line in the bed, and com-plained, "Your pajamas are touching my pajamas!" Many a "neatnik" has been paired with a "messy." Often sisters long for their own space and their own identity. Jan Kiemel Ream, twin sister of Ann Kiemel Anderson, writes in *Struggling for Wholeness*:

Sally with her new sister, Anne

> Ann and I had not only spent nine months in the womb together but eighteen years in the same bed-room.... I honestly didn't know who "I" was. I probably knew better who Ann was. I had never walked out the door without her approval on what I was wearing and didn't know even how to roll my own hair.[3]

When we adopted five-year-old Anne from an orphanage in Korea, I envisioned her sharing a bedroom with our eleven-year-old daughter, Sally (who is named after my sister Sally). At first, Sally was very excited to have a new little sister.

However, my visions of sugarplums and sweetness went awry when Sally was overcome, not with tender sister feel-ings, but with rivalry. Articulately, she explained to me that she did not enjoy sharing a room with Anne, "Everybody thinks Anne is so darling! You can't possibly understand my pain because you were always the baby. You can't imagine what it's like to be the baby for eleven years and then to be rudely displaced. I don't want to sleep next to her. Her breathing bugs me."

My husband and I prayed fervently for Sally and Anne's relationship. Each situation is different, which is why we need the Spirit's guidance. First, I realized that the shared bedroom might not be the best idea. Just as girls who are friends may need a time of space from each other, I realized that can be true with sisters. So we fixed up a room in the basement for Sally, wallpapering and painting to her specifications. We also showered Sally with love and patience.

In our situation, we realized Sally was really hurting, and when she couldn't sleep and eat, we took her for medical help. This is when we discovered Sally had a chemical imbalance and needed antidepressants.

People who are born with a chemical imbalance may not discover it until they face their first real stressful life situation. Most people release endorphins in stress—but some don't. It turned out that Sally was one of those. And though it may sound shocking to some to hear that we put a twelve-year-old on an antidepressant, it was exactly what Sally needed because she *does* have a chemical imbalance.

I cheer when speaker Kathy Troccoli, who also experienced a dramatic change when she was treated for chemical imbalance, says:

> Antidepressant is not a dirty word! I'm not talking about popping a pill when you are blue. But some of us were born with an imbalance, and just as diabetics need insulin, we need antidepressants to make our bodies work right. These are God's gifts to us. They clear the fog so we can then make the right choices.

When Sally's fog cleared, she realized her sin in not loving her sister. She asked God to change her heart, and He did. In time, great healing took place, and Sally often invited an excited Anne to come down and spend the night with her.

The night before Sally left for college, she crawled up into Anne's top bunk and held her. Anne said to her, "You know what, Sally?"

"What, Annie?"

"You are my very best friend."

As a young woman, Sally often spoke to teen groups and shared openly about the terrible year in which she felt "displaced" by Anne:

> Pain can have a refining work in us. When pain came into my life, I had to get help. Not only did I get medical help, I needed spiritual help. I practically ran to the front when a Christian singing group came to our local auditorium and gave an altar call. God revealed to me that my attitude was selfishness. When I repented and pleaded with Him to take the "yuk" out of my heart, He did! Not all at once, but slowly. I remember going to see the movie *Little Women* with Annie. As we watched the deep bond between those sisters, I was so thankful God had given me a sister. We cried buckets when Beth died. What would we do, we thought, without each other?

If your children are plagued with rivalry, get on your knees and pray, for we belong to a God who bends down and listens. The irritating sand of rivalry may bring forth a pearl—if you pray.

One of the comforts of adult sisterhood is getting past those mercurial years when your relationship fluctuates between warm intimacy and a glacial gap. The gap between me and my sisters seemed enormous all through childhood. They were six and four when I was born, and I was the invader, the pesky little sister who was always tattling, meddling, and intruding.

I remember the day the gap closed. I became very ill one night when my parents were gone, and Bonnie, who was about fourteen, was in charge. She was so concerned, calling the doctor and a neighbor, and getting me to the hospital emergency room. The warm feeling welling up inside of me wasn't just fever—it was the realization that my sister loved me.

My memories of magical moments were during that period when my sisters opened their circle and drew me in. Some of my best memories are from the summer when we shared beds in a loft in our log cabin. With our parents talking below, the sound of the waves on the beach, and the light of the fire flickering against the wall, Sally, the eldest, mentored us.

She whispered lessons on popularity, "When you get to high school, you will change classrooms between each period. When you pass people in the hall, smile, and say their names. Look right in their eyes and say, enthusiastically, 'Hi Susie!' and 'Hi, John!' This will help you be popular!"

We soaked it in, and vowed to do as our sister, the Homecoming Queen, instructed.

Our log cabin was plagued with bats, which Sally told us could get tangled in our hair. I can remember sleeping under the sheet like spoons with Bonnie, my smaller body tucked into her protective one. I felt loved, cared for, and shielded.

Shared Memories

One night when my parents were out, Sally narrated Edgar Allan Poe's "The Tell-Tale Heart" with great dramatic flair. Soon we were hearing noises everywhere. To protect ourselves, we got out the metal marshmallow sticks that hung in a rack next to the fireplace. When our parents returned late that night, they opened the door to find their three daughters poised, ready to plunge those metal sticks into an intruder's telltale heart.

Patti and Cynthia Clawson used to pretend they were Roy Rogers and Trigger. Cynthia was Trigger (because that was the more powerful part) and Patti would put a rope in her mouth and lead her around the backyard. (Cynthia says, "That's probably why I have capped teeth today.")

One of the conversations we often have at dinnertime is a sharing of memories, for in the telling and retelling, bonds are cemented. Likewise, bringing out the family movies and photo albums strengthens sibling bonds.

Shared Mother Stories

My sisters and I often swap "mother stories" when we are together. Last summer we remembered how Mother, a gifted soprano, would break into "Oh, What a Beautiful Morning" when we were out walking. We would all shrink several steps behind her. At this rewriting, our mother is ninety-three and we have been told she is dying, so we are taking turns holding vigil at her bedside, sharing new mother stories. Always the lady, always the hostess, she smiles weakly at each visitor. A twenty-two-year-old male aide came in to help shift her so she doesn't get bedsores. She surprised him and us by saying, "Where's my goodnight kiss?" She will be a flirt to the end.

Mother stories bond us together. No one knows our mother like we do—and we are proud that we are related to such a creative and dazzling woman! And when one of us says to the other, "You are sounding just like Mother," we burst into laughter, knowing precisely what that means, and secretly proud that we, like Mother, will never be boring.

Author Anne Ortlund says that her mother was intensely a lady and instructed her daughters in proper protocol, grooming, and manners. Anne writes of an experience she had with her sisters as adults: "We three sisters were in Washington, sitting on the grass watching a parade. It's been almost a half a century since Mother dressed us, but we discovered that for all our casual cottons, we had on skirts—and panty hose. We looked at one another, laughed, and acknowledged, 'Mother!'"[4]

Shared Spiritual Strength

My sister Sally led me to Christ when I was a young mother. Sally had come to Christ a year before through the influence of Campus Crusade for Christ. God impressed on Sally's heart in October of 1966 that I was more open to spiritual things than I had been in the past, and that she should travel to Indiana and lift up the claims of Christ. Though it was not a convenient time for her, she obeyed—and I am eternally grateful that she did.

Bonnie, Dee, & Sally as adults

Jennie Dimkoff, Carol Kent's younger sister, tells of walking out to the hayloft when she was seven, overwhelmed with doubts about her salvation: "I heard a noise and saw Carol, who was eleven, up in the hay mound having her devotions. To see her privately and quietly spending time with God was a real testimony to me. I climbed up next to her and poured out all my doubts and fears about my soul and she said, 'Jennie, just to be sure, let's pray together.' And she prayed with me, and from that day on I had assurance."

Jennie also tells of sharing a bedroom with Carol and of kneeling in prayer with her at night. "One prayer we prayed repeatedly was that others would be able to see Jesus on our faces. As adults, Carol and I began ministering together by singing at a retreat. Afterwards a woman came up and said, 'I can see Jesus on your faces.' The memory of our prayer as little girls came back instantly. And since that time there have been countless times people have told us that. God honored our prayer as children, and He continues to bond us together as adults."

Shared Sorrow

Because siblings have more years together than any other relatives, they are bound to share sorrow—for life is full of sorrow.

The Barrett Sisters, a black Gospel team, have sung together for over thirty years. When Delois's fourteen-year-old daughter became ill with hepatitis and was suffering tremendously, Delois said, "The three of us joined hands around the bed and asked the Lord to quiet her down. We told God it was all right to take her and asked Him to let her slip away, and that's exactly what the Lord did."[5]

Bennie Wiley is the younger and only sister of Sharon Pratt Dixon, a former mayor of Washington, D.C. When Sharon was four and Bennie two, their father told them the news that their mother had died. He asked his daughters to promise him that they would "look out for each other, stick together, and never let anything or anyone come between them." Bennie says, "I remember the strength in Sharon's eyes ... and from that day on, Sharon assumed responsibility for me. We have always been constant in each other's lives."[6]

When I lost my fifty-nine-year-old husband, my sister Bonnie was with me when he passed into eternity. She saw him lock eyes with me at the end and try to say, "I love you." She and Sally have been there for me through this hardest of years: praying for me, crying with me, e-mailing me, and holding up my weary arms. My sisters are so precious to me.

Most sisters are good friends, and a few become best friends. Yet rivalry is an underlying current in most sister relationships. For most, it's mild. For some, it's severe—and, as it was for Rachel and Leah of Genesis, their rivalry can be the obsession of their lives. Some sisters never grow up. They squabble until death parts them.

Is it really possible to completely outgrow sibling rivalry?

THE SIBLING BOND

Reflections

Action Points

CAN YOU EVER OUTGROW SIBLING RIVALRY?

Parents who continually overvalue one child provide the fuel for long-lasting sibling rivalry, even, "reaching back from the grave."

—STEPHEN BANK

Stephen P. Bank and Michael D. Kahn, *The Sibling Bond* (New York: Basic Books, 1982), 57.

CHAPTER 6

CAN YOU EVER OUTGROW SIBLING RIVALRY?

ost parents, when conceiving their children, don't project what their children's lives will be like in sixty years. Yet according to Dr. Stephen Bank and Dr. Michael Kahn, authors of *The Sibling Bond*, siblings provide a highly supportive network in old age, when parents and spouses have died, and children have gone their separate ways. The authors write:

> The decision made by a twentieth-century parent to have only one child can have consequences for life. In the twenty-first century the loneliest person in the world may well be the aged, unmarried only child who has no children and no siblings to love or be loved by.[1]

The sibling bond tends to be much more enduring than most friendships. Only 3 percent of siblings permanently disconnect. Jan, a young professional woman, describes what her siblings meant to her during the death of her mother: "It was a great comfort to be with my older brother and sister, to be with the people grieving the same loss I was. I had a real sense of going through that family crisis together. And a week later, when Christmas came, I realized that even with my mother gone (the woman who 'made' Christmas for us all), I still had family to come home to. And I know we'll continue to get together even after my father dies. At times like this, I'm glad I'm not an only child."

Yet many who are blessed with siblings do not relate well to them. To be related, yet not to be able to relate, brings frustration and grief. Experts say that failure to overcome rivalry separates siblings more than any factor.

Rivalry, in the Latin, means "having rights to the same stream." For siblings, that stream is the parents' love and approval. When I was pregnant with our second child, I feared, as is common with mothers, that I might not love my second child as much as my first. My love for my firstborn was so over-whelming that I feared there might not be enough love left in my heart for another. Yet when Johnny was born, my love welled up and overflowed. And today, as the mother of five, I believe that if God gives you a child, He also supplies plenty of love for each child.

However, some parents play favorites because of emo-tional problems of their own. Carolyn Koons, who was raised in an abusive home, felt the force of her father's hatred because he knew he was not her biological father. Every time he looked at her, he was reminded of his wife's infidelity. One year he bought her brothers new bikes for their birthdays and then went to the dump to find the worst bike he could to give to Carolyn.

If a parent plays favorites, the deprived children are impacted severely. Ginny, who checks my groceries, slid my food over the scanner a week before Christmas and vented her emotion: "I hate the holidays. My parents not only loved my brother best growing up, they still do. When we go home, he'll have the spot-light. His kids will get elaborate gifts. Mine will get socks. And yet I keep going home, hoping it will be different."

If you grew up in a family where parents played favorites, your challenge is greater—but not insurmountable.

Overcoming the Pain of Favoritism

Jacob and Esau were victims of parental favoritism and suffered enormously. Esau articulates that pain when he discovers that his father has given his blessing to his brother and cries, weeping: "Bless me—me too, my father!" (Genesis 27:34).

In *The Blessing,* Gary Smalley and John Trent say that Esau's anguished cry is being echoed today by many: "Some will try to break down the door to their parents' hearts to receive this missed blessing, but all too often their attempt fails. For whatever reason, they have to face the fact that their blessing will have to come from another source."[2]

Sometimes parental favoritism is perceived rather than real. As a mother of five, I know how difficult it is to treat each child equally. After we adopted Anne, I searched the catalogs for a Christmas stocking. I was delighted to find one that matched the style of our other children's stockings! However, when it arrived, Sally held it up to her own and found Anne's to be two inches longer. Accusingly she turned to me and asked, "Why is Anne's stocking bigger?" My patience ran thin, and Sally still remembers that I reacted by saying, "Give me a break!"

My husband helped me to see that, even if a child's feelings of being slighted are imagined, it is best to treat her fears with respect or you may aggravate the rivalry. During that difficult year of Sally's adjustment, Steve told me repeatedly, "Even though Sally's fears of losing our love are unreasonable, they don't feel that way to her. If we are patient, I think she'll get past it, and I think the dividend will be that she and Anne will be close."

He was right. I have become more compassionate toward the child who feels the loss of losing the limelight, even though it is temporary. Author Adrianne Rich said, "When my sister was born, it was like losing the Garden of Eden." A child's whole world is his or her parents' love, and it is a shock suddenly to have to share it.[3]

Most children are favored for a temporary period, and that is not necessarily wrong. A wise parent keeps communicating that this perceived favoritism is temporary, and keeps showering love on the child who is hurting.

Carol Kent told me, "My brother Ben was born in the middle of the night. After four girls, Dad was euphoric. He ran up the stairs to our big second-story bedroom, waking us with his shout: 'It's a boy! It's a boy! And Benjamin means SON OF MY RIGHT HAND!'"

Yet despite the fact that Ben seemed, at least for the time, to be the favored child, the sisters felt joy, not rivalry. Both felt loved and cherished and was therefore able to rejoice in their brother's birth.

Rivalry is natural but not desirable. I still have greater feelings of rivalry toward my sisters than I do toward my friends. When Bonnie's children went to Yale and Harvard, I felt a tremor of jealousy and dallied with the temptation to encourage my children to go to Ivy League schools. I am so thankful that knowing Christ and His Word helps me to veer away from choices based on rivalry.

Outgrowing sibling rivalry helps us make better choices for our lives, but, more than that, it fills our lives with a richness of relationship that is likely to last into old age.

Here are some ways that have been helpful to me and to others in putting away childish ways.

Admitting Feelings of Envy

Counselor Tara Markey believes that talking about childhood feelings is essential for healing: "You have to let down your guard. It becomes a trust issue—trust that you aren't going to hurt me like you did when I was a kid."[4]

A few years ago I admitted to my sisters my feelings of envy about not being a homecoming queen, and our conversation brought great healing to me. Bonnie said, "I certainly hope that becoming homecoming queen is not going to be my ultimate achievement in life." We laughed and I began to look at that time, not with pain, but with perspective and with humor.

Ann Kiemel's twin sister, Jan Ream, honestly shared that while Ann had all the fame of an author and speaker, Jan at least felt she excelled in the area of marriage and motherhood. In *Struggling for Wholeness*, Jan writes:

> When Ann married Will Anderson, it brought with it the most traumatic pain I had ever felt. It was during their honeymoon when I finally realized the bottom of my pain lay in the fact that ... she had seemingly always beaten me in any task we set out to conquer.... Now she was entering those two turfs [marriage and mother-hood] and she would certainly supersede me again.[5]

For Ann and Jan, much healing has come about simply because they have been willing to admit their rivalry. Jan says,

> For years I denied that I ever competed with Ann. But today I ashamedly admit that the feelings are there. In reality, if women were honest, all would confess to it.... I don't think we ever get rid of the struggle and pain of unhealthy competing.... Rather I think our freedom comes when we can confess it.[6]

Looking for God's Approval

Jennie Dimkoff says that people often marvel that she doesn't feel jealous of her sister, Carol Kent. Jennie and Carol have parallel lives in many ways, including the fact that they each speak to women's groups nearly every weekend—but Carol's star is higher right now than is Jennie's.

I was deeply moved by what Jennie told me: "I've pondered the story of Miriam—and of how, though she was gifted, she was still critical and jealous of her specially anointed brother, Moses. And God punished her (see Numbers 12). After that, the only thing we are told about Miriam is to 'remember what ... God did to Miriam' (Deuteronomy 24:9). Actually, what we do remember is her standing by the reeds watching Moses in his basket, or dancing with a tambourine after the parting of the Red Sea. But God tells us to remember how she was jealous and how He punished her.

"When I look at Carol, not only is she my best friend and my kindred spirit, but God has especially anointed her. There have been times when I sit back in awe at what God is doing through her. And it makes me cry. It would be so sinful and wrong to be jealous of her."

It grieves God when we cannot be content with how He has gifted us, but instead covet the gifts of a sibling. Karen Mains and Valerie Bell are gifted sisters who work closely together on "The Chapel of the Air," and do it well. Once, on the broadcast, Karen said:

> Eric Liddell, the hero of *Chariots of Fire,* said that he ran because God made him fast, and he felt God's pleasure when he ran. When we feel the intimate pleasure of God, it doesn't matter how He chooses to work with our brothers and sisters.[7]

Show Your Siblings How Much You Care

In Proverbs 21:14 we're told that a gift can soothe anger. When Jacob returned home, a mature and broken man, he was eager to reconcile with Esau. The gifts that he sent ahead were his way of apologizing and expressing love to the brother he had wronged.

It's amazing how much healing the expression of love provides. Bonnie, the sister closest to my age, was my greatest rival. Bonnie showed me how much she cared for me by flying to Nebraska and organizing a surprise twenty-fifth wedding anniversary celebration for Steve and me. There were many toasts that weekend, but the one I'll never forget was from

Bonnie. With her eyes flooding with tears, she raised her glass of juice and said, "Dee, I want you to know how very, very precious you are to me and how much I love you." It's amazing how that toast melted away nearly all of my rivalry!

In addition to longing for a "blessing" from our parents, most of us long for a "blessing" from our siblings as well. We want to know that we are loved and special in their eyes. After adopting Anne, we then adopted a girl from Thailand, who was a year older than Anne. Shortly after we brought Beth home, we found Anne upstairs weeping on her bed. The pain she was feeling that day was not only from the fact that we, her parents, had been giving Beth extra attention, but that Sally, Anne's big sister, had had Beth in her room trying on clothes all evening. The next morning Sally took Anne (and only Anne) out for doughnuts before school as a way of saying, "I love you, Anne—always."

Affirming Your Siblings

Carol Kent told me, "I think it's really important to look at your siblings and find something that they do well and brag on it. Most human beings, especially women, suffer from low self-esteem. You could have been raised in the best Christian family possible and still be struggling with feelings of inadequacy. When my first book came out, my four sisters celebrated with me, through letters and calls! Jennie carried my books to her speaking engagements and told people, 'This is the best book I've ever read in my whole life and you need to get it today.'"

Outgrowing sibling rivalry is a worthwhile pursuit. Jan Senn, who described herself as "the brat little sister who always interrupted the boyfriends in the basement to iron my ribbons," has made peace with her older brother and sister. Today, they're helping each other fill the gap that the loss of their mother has created. Reflectively, Jan said, "Mom was Karen's best friend, and they'd spend hours just talking on the phone, but Karen and I always had a purpose when we talked to each other. After Mom's death, however, Karen called me and was chatting on and on, and I kept thinking, *What's the point of this call?* and then a warm feeling welled up inside me as I realized there wasn't a point. She just wanted to talk."

There is so very much to be gained by outgrowing sibling rivalry.

Likewise, there is much to be gained by putting away childish ways in our friendships.

After I spoke at "The Changed Life Seminar" near Toledo about "Putting Away Childish Ways," a threesome came up to me. A pretty brunette in the middle was the first to speak, thanking me profusely for thoughts I had shared. The young woman on her left said, "This has been a very challenging retreat! A painfully maturing one!"

I raised my eyebrows—I wanted further explanation!

The woman in the middle hugged the friend who'd made herself vulnerable and explained, "Lilly didn't think you could have more than one best friend."

I smiled as I suddenly realized the significance of the threesome.

Three doesn't work very well with little girls—but it should work with women. It's time to learn to put away childish ways in friendship. Next, let's consider how to make a threesome work.

CAN YOU EVER OUTGROW SIBLING RIVALRY?

Reflections

Action Points

THE TRIANGLE

Maybe it's crazy, but when my best friend began to pull away a little, I felt more like a jilted lover than a friend who'd been knocked down a notch or two in importance. It wasn't good enough to be just one of her close friends, not after what we shared for so many years.

—A FIFTY-YEAR-OLD WOMAN FROM *JUST FRIENDS*

Lillian Rubin, *Just Friends* (New York: Harper and Row, 1985), 188.

CHAPTER 7

THE TRIANGLE

*T*hough nearly a half century has passed, the tearful scene between Judy, the new girl in my fifth grade, and Donna and me, who were best friends, is indelibly impressed on my guilty heart.

I was drawn to Judy the moment Miss Kolander introduced her to our class. She looked just like one of my dolls: wispy black curls framing a petite porcelain face with huge blue eyes—and she dimpled when she smiled, which was often.

When Judy called me that week and asked if I could come and spend the night with her on Friday, I was elated to be the chosen one! And I was not disappointed. We roasted hot dogs and marshmallows in her family-room fireplace and sat on a blanket while I told her all about who was nice and who wasn't in the fifth grade. That night we whispered and giggled under the covers until it was very late, savoring the joy of friendship discovered.

But Donna was my best friend and Donna was angry that I had spent the night at Judy's. Donna threw down the gauntlet: I had to choose. I couldn't have them both. I chose

Donna—because Donna had been my best friend for two years. We were a constant in each other's lives: We played at every recess, walked home together every night, and talked on the phone when we were apart. I didn't think I could survive without Donna.

I was forced to let Judy know my decision on Monday when she caught up with Donna and me after school. Her deep dimples and sparkling blue eyes told me she was unsuspecting of the treachery that was coming. I can still remember where we stood on the sidewalk outside of McClain Grade School when Donna announced, "Dee and I are going to walk home together."

"But can't I walk with you too?" asked Judy.

Hesitantly, I replied, "I'm sorry."

"But I thought we were getting to be good friends!" exclaimed Judy.

I paused. I felt so torn! Donna took my hand possessively. "Judy, I really am sorry—but Donna is my best friend."

"My mother says that three girls can be good friends. Can't we all be friends?" asked Judy.

My concern was rising. Judy's mother had been wonderful to me on Friday night, telling me she was so glad Judy had such a nice little friend. Donna, sensing my vacillating heart, stepped dramatically forward, placing herself between Judy and me.

"Judy, you can't have more than one best friend! Dee and I were best friends before you ever came here. So you have to find a different best friend."

"Dee?" Judy's lip was trembling now. She looked at me beseechingly as Donna turned and cast me a warning look.

Cowardly, I responded, "Donna is my best friend."

Defeated, Judy cried, "I hate you both! You are both so mean! I never want to play with you again!" She fled, in tears.

I would like to tell you that when I became a woman I put away childish ways—but I was in my thirties before I clearly saw the sin in territorial friendships. (And wherever you are, Judy— please forgive me!)

I'd like to share with you some of the ways God has changed my thinking.

The New Kid on the Block

When I was growing up, my parents never moved. I spent my first eighteen years in the same house on Highland View Drive in West Bend, Wisconsin. I was never the new kid on the block—and, as you can see from the story above, I was not particularly compassionate toward her plight!

After I married, however, Steve and I moved eight times because each new venture of his medical training or time in the Public Health Service took him to a different region of the United States. I quickly learned what it meant to be the new kid, looking in on those who were content in their existing network of friendships!

God, in His grace, didn't treat me as I had treated others in my childhood. When we moved to Fargo, North Dakota, I prayed for a soul mate—as I had learned to do! I was doing interviews for a writing project, and one of the most interesting women I interviewed was Ann Dahl. I was immediately attracted to her depth and warmth, and we had an interchange that day that made me feel she might be the friend for whom I longed. Something I said caused Ann to smile and say: "You sound a bit like an evangelical feminist! Are you?"

Like a diver who's reluctant to dive into untested waters, I paused. Quickly I reassured my new acquaintance that I was pro-life, pro-family, and pro-male! Smiling empathetically, she said: "I'm somewhere between Marabel Morgan's *Total Woman* and Letha Scanzoni's *All We're Meant to Be.*"

I suddenly sensed, as Anne of Green Gables is fond of saying, "a kindred spirit." She was a reader, a ponderer! I laughed and said, "I'm somewhere in there too!" Then I freely shared some of the concepts I had learned from various authors who held the high view of Scripture, yet felt that some Christian views of marriage and of ministry failed to appreciate that God intended women to be active participants.

Ann was familiar with those authors, and we began finishing each other's sentences. I shared the pain I had felt in one denomination when I realized that women were not welcome to share their thoughts in Sunday school class. Ann was completely compassionate. We experienced the joy of seeing our friendship sprout before our very eyes.

A few months later, Ann told me that her very best friend from the past was moving from Florida to Fargo! Though I smiled on the outside, I was sure this new friendship, which had sprung up so quickly, was in danger of being crowded out in its infancy, before it had a chance to grow strong and tall.

Ann raved about Sylvia and her husband, Kendall, who was coming to work with Ann's husband. Kendall and Howie had been close since their days together at Trinity Seminary. Not only were Sylvia and Ann soul mates, their husbands were as well! I felt the cold wind approaching: Sylvia and Ann would be as snug as bugs in a rug—and I would be outside, shivering in the bitter Fargo winter!

But that isn't what happened. Ann also raved to Sylvia about me and arranged for the three of us to have lunch together. Sylvia didn't seem threatened by me in the least, just terribly eager to meet me. Our time together that day was one of the most special fellowships in my memory. Sparks went from one to another as we sharpened one another with our understanding of Scripture and of thoughts from various Christian authors. Laughter abounded. Afterward we walked and prayed together—experiencing the joy of a threefold cord.

Helping Each Other Find Strength in God

Author Gail McDonald helped me to see a key verse in the friendship of David and Jonathan. When David was hiding at Horesh, in fear of being murdered by King Saul, Jonathan went to him and "helped him find strength in God" (1 Samuel 23:16). Gail asked, "Do you help your friend find strength in you? Or in God?" How wise Jonathan was! Shortly after this he was killed in battle, but David was not abandoned, for his strength was in God.

I believe that Jonathan helped David find strength in God by praying with him, by encouraging him with Scripture, and by sharing the way he saw God working. This kind of friendship was the kind of friendship I experienced with Ann and Sylvia. Rather than behaving like little girls, guarded and territorial concerning their best friend, they opened their circle. They were convinced that God was leading the three of us to be friends. And when we got together, we helped each other find strength, not in each other, but in God.

Our friendship was healthy, edifying, and satisfying. I knew that Ann and Sylvia would always be closer to each other than either was to me, because their friendship had such deep roots. But I was deeply grateful that they had opened their circle and drawn me in. If I spent time with one and not the other, there was no jealousy—just delight in our threefold cord!

When we parted a year later (because Steve and I moved to Nebraska), though it was painful, it wasn't devastating. God was going with me—and I felt He would provide me with soul mates in Nebraska as He had in Fargo. My security was not in Ann and Sylvia, but in God.

One spring I was giving a retreat in Florida, and Sylvia (who now lives in Florida) and Ann came. After my last session, we headed to Daytona Beach for a walk along the ocean. As it happened, it was also "Bikers' Week"—so it wasn't quite the peaceful setting we had envisioned. Along with swooping seagulls and lapping waves were roaring motorcyclists. Yet the rumble of the motors didn't keep us from connecting. We shouted to be heard, and grinned—grins born not only of the humor of our situation, but of the deep joy of being reunited and of helping one another once again find strength in God.

Though we now live in three different states, I have stayed in touch with Ann and Sylvia. However, as the years passed, we basically became "Christmas-card friends." But when Steve died, I also lost a friend that edified me like no other friend had.

We would pray and talk in the night about spiritual things. When I had questions on predestination, he challenged me to read Luther's *Bondage of the Will;* when I wondered if President George W. Bush was right to invade Iraq, he said I couldn't really be articulate about it until I read *The Clash of Civilizations.* Steve prayed through the psalms with me and introduced me to Spurgeon's *Treasury of David.*

One day I was missing the way Steve would challenge me to read more than fiction. It occurred to me that at this new stage of my life, as a young widow with such a gaping hole in my life, it might be wise to reassess my friendships. I treasured each friend I had, but I had some new needs.

I needed reading friends who would challenge me, as Steve had, and I needed friends who could be free to be with me at times without their husbands. They either needed to be single themselves or be married to, as Jan Silvious has described so well, "an anchor rather than a ball and chain." I knew that both Ann and Sylvia had husbands who were *not* a ball and chain. In fact, Howie and Kendall would *encourage* Ann and Sylvia to spend time with me. I decided to try to fan the glowing embers of our friendship into a flame that would warm us all.

I e-mailed Sylvia first, telling her I was going to be speaking in Florida. Would she come? Could I spend some time with her? She did, and we connected as though no time had passed at all.

Four months later I was in Florida again, and this time, I spent three extra days at Sylvia's. We discussed Reformed theology, the war in Iraq, being a good mother-in-law, and Bible studies that had been particularly edifying. Afterwards, in my thank-you note, I told her I was serious about wanting to rekindle our friendship. We began praying for one another through e-mail and calling one another on our cell phones. I also asked her to come to Wisconsin to spend time with me at my cabin. She agreed, and so I invited Ann, too.

I smiled to see that I was rewriting *this* chapter, talking about *this* sweet triangle friendship, on the eve of Ann and Sylvia's arrival.

Ann arrived first and we had supper on the back porch, watching the September sun sink into Green Bay. We started talking about books. Ann said, "Have you read Lauren Winter's *Girl Meets God?*"

"Oh, I just read it this summer! I've memorized my favorite part:

> Sometimes, as in a great novel, you cannot see until you get to the end that God was leaving clues for you all along. Sometimes you wonder, "How did I miss it? Surely any idiot should have been able to see from the second chapter that it was Miss Scarlet in the conservatory with the rope."

Ann laughed. "You make me want to read it again!"

And off we went, helping one another find strength in God.

Sylvia is a reader as well and when she arrived it was with a book by Steve Brown called *Scandalous Freedom*, and she read aloud from it, giving us wisdom for overcoming. Both Sylvia and I have had someone in our lives who is hurting a loved one deeply, and we talked about *how* to forgive—and we prayed for grace to forgive.

One of the things I appreciate in Sylvia is her desire to be conformed to Christ. She humbly told me about a few of the times in the last few months when she needed "an attitude check," and the Lord transformed her thinking.

When Sylvia arrived, the nearby care center where my mother lives called to tell me they thought Mother was in her last weeks. Sylvia, who lost both her mother and mother-in-law in the last two months, was the perfect friend to stand by my side. How good of God to be mindful of us for such a time as this.

A Cord of Three Strands

Because as women we have a tendency toward dependency, having two soul mates may be a safeguard. It's a bit too easy, when you have just one soul mate, to become all things to each other, and to put unreasonable demands on each other.

I feel that God has given me a "composite" soul mate. Because I have more than one soul mate, I am less demanding. When a friend needs space for family or ministry, I am more willing to give it. And when I need space, I feel less like I am abandoning my friends, for I know that they have other sources of emotional nurturing.

Solomon says, in Ecclesiastes 4:9, that two are better than one. He goes on in verse 12 to say, "Though one may be overpowered, two can defend themselves. A cord of three strands is not quickly broken."

While a cord of three strands is often likened to two friends and God (which is an apt analogy), there's also support here for having more than one soul mate. It is certainly healthier. One woman who has been delivered from a lesbian relationship called me to thank me for *The Friendships of Women* and its part in helping her.

She told me, "I always realized the sexual involvement was sin, but I didn't know how to be delivered. Your book helped me to see the root problem was dependency—we had transferred our dependency from God to each other."

This woman is back on track. To stay there, not only does she need to keep her love relationship with the Lord alive, she needs to be on guard about becoming dependent on any one woman ever again. One of the best ways to do that is by having more than one close friend. In the newest edition of *The Friendships of Women* I have some wonderful new stories of women who were delivered, not from lesbianism, but from dependent friendships. One of the women, Christy, tells how she could become physically ill if she didn't hear from a particular friend—but it was her other friends who got around her and said, "This isn't good, Christy. This isn't healthy. Please get help." Christy did, and today is so thankful to be free.

I have also counseled many a young wife that she needs to have other close friends in addition to her husband. Expecting a husband to be "all things" to you can be damaging to your marriage.

But what do you do if your husband is threatened by your friendships?

The Triangle

Reflections

Action Points

HUSBANDS VERSUS BEST FRIENDS

CHAPTER 8

HUSBANDS VERSUS BEST FRIENDS

Most men do not have a same-sex confidante. The exceptions tend to be right-brained males or spiritual giants. But generally speaking, men do not confide in other men. If they confide, they confide in a woman—generally, their wives. So many men wonder, since they are content to have their only close friend be their spouse, why it can't be the same for women.

In the movie *Beaches,* Rosalie and Susan become friends in childhood and continue their very volatile friendship all through their lives. One day, after a particularly bitter fight, Rosalie is convinced she has lost Susan. Grieving, she says to her husband: "What will I do without a best friend?"

He says: "But you've got me!"

Rosalie shakes her head and stares out into the distance. "It's not the same," she says.

As women, we understand. We are not saying that we value our relationships with women more than our relationships with men, but that they are different—and we need both. Yet it's important to understand that our intimate relationship with our "sisters" can seem threatening to our husbands.

Psychotherapist Lillian Rubin interviewed husbands about their wives' friendships and found that many were mystified, particularly by the intensity of the friendship in the beginning. The aura of romance can seem threatening to the exclusivity of the marriage relationship. One man said:

> She thinks I don't like her friend Peg, but that's not it. (Uncomfortably) I guess maybe I'm jealous. When they first met, you'd think they were having some kind of love affair the way they were always trying to figure ways to get together and talking on the phone all the time. Why would I feel good about that?[1]

Sometimes husbands are justified in their concerns, for they *are* being neglected by their wives. We wouldn't want our husbands to be fishing with his buddies every weekend or on the phone every evening. Other times men simply need reassurance that intimacy between women is quite normal and has no reflection on our feelings for them.

Use Word Pictures

Peter urges husbands to "live with their wives in an understanding way" (1 Peter 3:7 NASB), but men will often admit they need help to do that. One man said, "I think she thinks I can read her mind—but I can't. It helps so much if she tells me what she is thinking."

Because most men are left-brained, word pictures will illuminate that dark right brain. Joan said, "I've explained to my husband that I have this fountain of words bubbling up from my heart, and if I used them all on him he might drown! He laughed, and I think he really does understand and is very supportive of my need to be with other women."

Just because we confide in other women does not mean that we do not also confide in our husbands. A study by P. O'Connor found that women who confide in other women also confide in their husbands. One does not preclude the other.[2] It might be helpful to express this to your husband and also to emphasize his uniqueness.

I love the picture of the body—the hand needs the eye, but it also needs the other hand. I could honestly tell Steve, "I do share my heart with Jean and Patti, and they often, because they are women as well, help me understand myself. The hand understands the hand. But there is a part of me I can share only with you—because you are my husband, and no one can be to me what you are. You are like the eye, or, even more aptly, the heart to me. Because we are one in every way, what we have is unique and sacred—and no one can fill that place for me but you."

Maturity Brings Understanding

Young husbands may feel more threatened than more mature husbands. As men observe women, they become more comfortable with the intimacy of our friendships. I loved the way Kathie Lee described a conversation she had with two women friends and her husband, Frank Gifford.

> The four of us began sharing our private thoughts on love and relationships.... Then the woman-talk got so emotionally intimate, so intense and deeply spiritual, that Frank got up. Guess he couldn't stand the heat so he went back to the kitchen—after sweetly clearing the dishes. "I'll just leave you ladies alone," he said.[3]

Sadly, though men may come to accept emotional closeness between women, they feel it is reserved for women or for a woman and a man. They can't imagine it for themselves with other men. They agree with *Newsweek* columnist Elliot Engel who, after watching the last hugs between his wife and her best friend before a cross-country move, concluded, sadly: "You've got to have a bosom to be a buddy."[4]

Do You Have to Have a Bosom to Be a Buddy?

In some cultures men do have close friends. Addy Mull, who is living in Africa, wrote to me: "Where I live, the men walk hand in hand, they kiss when they greet, and after a soccer game they will often agree that both teams won—because they feel that competition hinders intimacy."

If it can happen in Africa—why not America—why not everywhere?

The key, I believe, is the source of our identity. Women have an easier time being relational because their identity has always been in relationships. If you ask a woman to share a few sentences about herself, she will almost always mention her relationships. A man, however, will almost invariably mention his job, for a man's identity usually is in his position—his status. If a woman attempts suicide, it's commonly over the loss of a relationship—but if a man attempts suicide, it's more likely to be due to an injured sense of pride or competence, a perceived loss of status—often related to work.[5]

This helps me to understand why intimacy is hard for men, particularly with other men, for status and intimacy are opposites. If you make yourself vulnerable, you may lose status. If you show emotion, you may appear weak. If you ask for help, it indicates you can't do it by yourself.

So what is the solution? As men begin to find their identity in Christ, they become less fearful of intimacy and the barriers begin to fall. Spiritual giants tend to have close and rewarding friendships with other men. Consider David and Jonathan. Consider Jesus. He made Himself vulnerable—asking for help from His friends in the garden of Gethsemane. He showed emotion frequently—even weeping in public at the tomb of His friend Lazarus. His friendships with other men were deep and rewarding.

And this is exactly what is happening for men in America. Promise Keepers made an enormous impact in that area, and the evidence is strong that for many the results are lasting. Men are making themselves vulnerable to each other, praying together, and holding one another accountable to be true to their God and to their families.

One wife reported on the change in her husband after being to Promise Keepers: "He asked me to pray with him, and while we were praying, he wept. I could hardly believe it!"

How can we help our husbands grow spiritually? The most effective thing we can do is to pray, for James tells us the fervent prayer of a righteous man (or woman) is effective. And, if you are falling more deeply in love with Jesus, it will be contagious.

My daughter-in-law underwent a personal revival in her love relationship with Jesus recently. My son, John, said, "Julie can hardly wait to get up in the morning to get out of bed to go and spend time with Jesus. It makes me jealous to have what she has. I want to go deeper in my walk as well."

Be Wary of Friends Who Hurt Your Marriage

If a friend seems jealous of your time with your husband, or if she makes derogatory remarks about him, beware. Several years ago a woman I'll call Jenna began writing me about feeling caught between loyalty to her husband and loyalty to her best friend, Nicole.

> I have never connected with anyone the way I've con-nected with Nicole. And she's always been there for me, even to the extent of flying to Mexico when I was in a car accident and nursing me back to health.
>
> When I started dating Frank, she told me it was THE MISTAKE OF MY LIFE. I was hurt, but I loved him and thought Nicole would grow to appreciate him. She hasn't! Though I married him, Nicole still tells me, constantly, that God has someone better for me.

It was clear to me from Jenna's letters that she needed to risk losing Nicole if Nicole couldn't be supportive of her marriage.

Though Jenna seemed to realize that Nicole was hurting her perception of Frank, she lacked the courage and wisdom to take a stand. She wrote, wistfully, "I just can't lose Nicole. She's too important to me." When you have these kinds of feelings about a friend who may be destroying your marriage, your friendship is too important to you.

I believe that God in His grace intervened. Jenna couldn't call off the friendship, but after a particularly sharp disagreement, Nicole did it for her. Jenna wrote me during that time, her letters filled with pain. "I miss her so much," she wrote. "When will I stop hurting?" I knew, however, that now Jenna's marriage had a possible future.

Years later Jenna came to one of my retreats and sought me out. She told me that after Nicole retreated, she and Frank went to a Christian marriage counselor for sixteen months. In time, their marriage flourished. Reflectively, Jenna said:

> Though the pain of having my best friend turn from me was intense, I now see that God meant it for our good. We had become inordinately important to each other and the Lord had to shake up our priorities. Today we are exploring friendship again, but cautiously. Nicole knows I am committed to my marriage, and we each have other close friends.
>
> I now clearly see that any person outside of a marriage that encourages the breakup of a family unit without any scriptural basis is out of God's will. I am strong enough now to ask Nicole to respect my personhood and my relationship with the Lord enough to change her belief about Frank. If she can't, I will treasure my memories with her, but our friendship has no future.

There have been times when I have thought that my friends made a poor choice of a husband, but because I value the sanctity of marriage, I need to be supportive of that marriage! The only exception to this is when—because of a husband's substance abuse, physical abuse, or infidelity—you need to give your friend the support she needs to separate from him and exercise tough love, the kind of love that says, "I love you—but I will not tolerate this behavior. Therefore, we can't be together unless you get the help you need to make a genuine change." This kind of tough love is not anti-marriage, but pro-marriage, for boundaries must be set in order for the marriage to have any hope at all.

Supporting Your Friend's Marriage

As I shared in the opening chapter of this book, studies show that women's friendships generally enhance rather than hurt marriages. As Christians, that should be doubly true, because we know how highly God values the sanctity of marriage. It isn't our responsibility to point out the faults of our friend's husband.

But what do you do when it's your friend who is pointing out her husband's faults? Dr. Dobson asked me about this tricky situation when I was on "Focus on the Family." He said, "On the one hand, she needs to respect her husband—on the other hand, in a true friendship, she needs to be able to ventilate. What's the solution?"

I think we should be able to ventilate, but only to friends who understand the sanctity of marriage. And when a friend is ventilating to me, I must keep uppermost in my mind that I want the best for her, and the best is a response that will edify her marriage. Sometimes I can help diffuse emotion by letting her ventilate, sometimes I can help her to see his side, and sometimes I can help her see the humor in the situation.

One summer, Margaret and Larry and their three children stopped to visit me and our children at our summer place. (My husband had not yet joined us.) Larry, an administrator, is like many left-brained, goal-oriented men. He had scheduled their "vacation" tightly—they were going to "conquer" ten places in ten days! When the five of them arrived at our cabin (their fifth goal), I sensed the tension between Margaret and Larry.

I hurried them out to the dock to catch a glimpse of the scarlet sun slipping into the bay, because they planned to leave in the morning, and I thought it might be their only Door County sunset. When just a crimson hue remained, the chill drove us inside to the fire. Margaret collapsed in a big chair, but Larry was restless and decided to take the children miniature golfing.

Alone together, I empathized with my friend: "Marg, is your vacation wearing you out?"

"Oh, yes! We've been going so hard. I would love to take it easy, but Larry has all these goals he wants to accomplish!"

I laughed, hoping to defuse her tension with humor. I told her that Larry reminded me of my wonderful dad, who took months meticulously preparing for family trips and had every moment carefully scheduled.

While in his late seventies, Dad whirled my mother, Steve, and me through every corner of England and Scotland in ten days. I often was aware, during that trip, of the differences between men and women. Dad wanted us to see all the famous spots; Mother wanted to meander through the shops, sit down, have tea, and talk.

I was feeling somewhat frustrated about the trip until, one night, I saw my dad poring over his careful plans for the next day. My heart filled with love for him as I realized how hard he was working. The next day we let Mother and Steve rest at the hotel, while Dad and I explored Oxford together, seeing where C. S. Lewis taught and lunched and was buried. I told Margaret I cherished the memory of that joyous day with my dad—but I'd have missed it had God not helped me to see Dad's loving motives.

Margaret pensively poked at the fire. Smiling, she began reminiscing how she and Larry had reacted differently when their family was snowed in last winter.

"I absolutely love it when it snows so hard that Larry's office is closed and school is canceled. The family is cloistered together and the world is held at bay! When that happened last year,

Larry made a big fire, like this one, and I envisioned playing games with the kids with a big bowl of popcorn. I was delighted to see the snow piling up because the five of us would be cozy in our circle of love before the flickering fire. It would be just like a scene from *Little House on the Prairie.*

"Instead, Larry was excited about using his new snow blower. I suggested he wait until it stopped snowing and play a few games with us. But he just had to get out with his machine."

When Larry and the children returned, they found Margaret and I giggling. Taking his jacket off, Larry said, "I don't know if my ears are burning from the cold or because you two have been talking about me!"

We laughed at his discernment. I told him how much we appreciated the quiet time he'd given us together while he entertained the children. He responded, sensitively: "Well I think Margaret needed that."

I gave him an appreciative smile and said, "Marg and I are so blessed to have discerning husbands like you and Steve. You are right—Marg does need to unwind! And you are right that we've been talking about you—and about the differences between men and women in general!"

Larry raised his eyebrows. "I think I'd better hear this."

We laughed, and I attempted an explanation: "Well, I think God designed most men to be goal oriented, and most women to be relational—and sometimes that causes a bit of conflict! Like on days when the family is snowed in—or on vacations!"

Larry smiled good-naturedly, understanding my point. I seized the moment and said, "Larry, instead of getting back on the road tomorrow after breakfast, why not make it your goal to let Marg and the kids stop and catch their breath here! Call and cancel your reservations in Milwaukee. I'd absolutely love to have you for an extra day!"

The kids chorused, "Please, Dad!" Larry laughed, putting his hands up in mock defense: "Well, tell you what—I'll think about it."

The next day we were graced from above with glorious weather. Encouraged by the warmer weather and the sight of our children skipping pebbles together on a sunlit bay, I gingerly made my plea again. Larry set his breakfast coffee mug down and grinned: "OK—we'll stay!" We rejoiced and ran to tell the kids, who rejoiced with us!

Sitting in a deck chair was too sedentary for Larry, but Margaret and I stretched out while he and their sons paddled the canoe to Horseshoe Island. (One of Larry's goals was to get a rock from each place they visited, and he decided a rock from an island would add character to their collection!)

Margaret and I basked in the sun and watched her conquerors head for the island. We talked about how thankful we were to be married to conquerors, even though it could be frustrating. (Steve conquered medical school, our taxes, our leaking roof, and the red tape involved in adopting children from other countries.) I could also give Margaret hope (for we are older than they) because I watched Steve become much more relaxed and relational in his maturity.

When we saw Larry and the boys paddling home, we were concerned because the canoe was low in the water. We understood why when we saw the boulder they had retrieved for the rock collection. What a conquest! Marg and I couldn't stop laughing.

In her thank-you note, Margaret said the atmosphere of their vacation took a positive U-turn after their time at our summer place! How encouraged I felt to know I'd played a small part in strengthening their marriage!

Having a good, strong marriage isn't easy in this day of sexual infidelity, dual-career marriages, and quick divorces. However, we do have one advantage that wives in Old Testament days lacked. Most of us don't have to worry about sharing our husbands with another wife or two. Or do we?

HUSBANDS VERSUS BEST FRIENDS

Reflections

Action Points

CAN AN EX-WIFE AND A NEW WIFE GET ALONG?

I had lost my mate, and to some extent my social position. I know my wife-in-law [husband's new wife] is much better off financially than I am. She's the one taking the fancy trips and redecorating her home while I'm pinching pennies. But one thing I wasn't prepared for was my five-year-old daughter coming to me one day and saying, "Oh, Mommy, Mara makes the best fried chicken, and we had so much fun planting a garden together. I can't wait to go back next Saturday."

—ANN CRYSTER

Ann Cryster, *The Wife-in-Law Trap* (New York: Pocket Star Books, 1990), 30.

CHAPTER 9

CAN AN EX-WIFE AND A NEW WIFE GET ALONG?

*B*efore Christ came to earth, many a woman had to share her husband with another wife. But Jesus elevated the position of women and, for the next nineteen centuries, polygamy was rare.

In the middle of the twentieth century, however, divorce became first acceptable and then common. Today many women are faced with stress similar to that of their polygamous ancestors because of the contemporary practice of "serial" monogamy. Many women have become victims of divorce just as women in the past were victims of polygamy.

Ann Cryster has coined the term "wife-in-law" to describe the relationship between the ex-wife and the new wife. If you are not a "wife-in-law," you probably have a friend who is and who'd appreciate empathy and encouragement from you.

PAIN is what is expressed over and over again by ex-wives. The pain of the actual divorce is the beginning. But as long as her other half remains single, she has hope of reconciliation, of the healing of her gaping wound. That's why the news of a new wife is so devastating. One woman described the shock like this: "The news of my ex's new wife? It's like remembering where you were when Kennedy was shot."[1]

If you were the one who initiated the divorce, as was the case with a friend of mine, you may assume you can get him back if you choose. My friend kept telling me she was glad she had divorced her husband. I half-believed her until I saw how she reacted when he remarried. The reality that she could never have him back sent her reeling.

First meetings with the new wife are typically traumatic, says author Ann Cryster. She tells how one ex-wife felt the first time she met her husband's new wife, Trish.

> I was working around the house that afternoon. Hank, Trish, and the kids had been away for Labor Day, and they suddenly pulled into the driveway. After eight hours in the car, Trish hops out in perfectly pressed linen shorts with every hair on her head in place. I felt like Godzilla facing Venus. It was the first time I had seen them as a couple, a family. I thought I had a grip on it all, but when I went back into the house I cried for the entire night. I can't describe the loneliness, the unhappiness. I was convinced that no one would ever love me again. I felt used up, discarded and ridiculous.[2]

I imagine that those were some of the feelings that Leah had when, after one week with her new husband, she saw her beautiful younger sister, Rachel, invade her tent. If there is one word to describe the lives of Leah and Rachel, it is PAIN.

Leah: The Rejected Wife

Laban was a tricky dad who had a plan to get both of his daughters married off. Laban veiled his older daughter, Leah, heavily so that Jacob would think he was marrying her beautiful younger sister, Rachel. All night long Jacob thought he was making love to Rachel. (Did he murmur softly, "Rachel, oh, Rachel …"?) But when dawn broke and he looked upon the face of his sleeping bride, Jacob realized he'd been duped. He tore from their tent to confront Laban, shouting: "Give me my wife. My time is completed, and I want to lie with her" (Genesis 29:21).

Jacob had been humiliated in front of everyone. He probably felt like the laughingstock of Haran. And when Leah saw his reaction, she must have felt mortified, discarded.

Laban tried to placate Jacob, saying, "It is not our custom here to give the younger daughter in marriage before the older one. Finish this daughter's bridal week; then we will give you the younger one also, in return for another seven years of work" (Genesis 29:26–27).

So Leah had Jacob to herself for one week—a week in which he pined for Rachel.

When Rachel moved into their tent a week later, perhaps Leah fantasized that, after Jacob knew Rachel as she did, he wouldn't be so smitten. But he was. Throughout his life he adored Rachel. Even when Rachel was barren, Jacob loved her. And when she finally gave birth to Joseph, he was Jacob's favorite son, setting off ripples of sibling rivalry. Oh, the pain Leah endured all her life!

A friend of mine whom I will call Penny was just twenty-five when her husband of four years left her and their three-year-old daughter, Molly, for another woman. Penny confided in me often during those painful years, and I see real parallels with her and Leah.

Penny said, "I wanted Matt to be miserable with Brooke. I hoped she'd be a nag and unresponsive in bed. I know that's terrible—but that's what I wanted. He had hurt us so badly—I wanted him to hurt too.

"When Molly would spend weekends with Matt and Brooke, I'd pump her for details. I know you are not supposed to do that to a child, but I did. I was so curious to see if my hopes were being fulfilled. One time Molly told me something that left me furious, humiliated, and heartbroken.

"Matt and Brooke had taken her camping. Apparently they thought she was asleep, because they made love with her next to them in the tent. Molly told me, 'I think Daddy was hurting Brooke because she kept moaning.'

"I called Matt and told him what I thought about his indiscreet behavior with Molly. He apologized profusely and I think he did feel bad. What he couldn't apologize for was loving Brooke more than he did me. I've cried buckets about that."

Leah must have cried buckets in her life. She had to watch Jacob's eyes light up when Rachel appeared; she had to watch him pull her sister tenderly to himself and whisper to her; and she had to sleep alone while Jacob was in the bedroom of her beautiful sister.

The Lord was compassionate toward Leah's plight: "When the LORD saw that Leah was not loved, he opened her womb, but Rachel was barren" (Genesis 29:31).

Leah spent years longing for her husband's love. She hoped that giving him sons would win his love. When she gave birth to her firstborn son, Reuben, she said, "Surely my husband will love me now" (Genesis 29:32). She had three more sons, and each time hoped that this child would turn her husband's heart toward her. But it didn't.

Meanwhile, while four little boys clung to Leah's skirt, Rachel was barren. And Rachel was vexed by her sister's fertility.

Rachel: The New Wife

The new wife's life is not necessarily a bed of roses. When Ann Cryster interviewed second wives, she found many were insecure in their husband's love. For one thing, they knew he was capable of breaking his marriage vows. In addition, many saw evidence that he still had feelings of affection for his first wife. Cryster writes, "Even though she [the new wife] has the license and the ring, she feels that the competition will never end. At the back of her mind lurks the fear that her husband still pines for his ex-wife, even more attractive now that she is forbidden fruit."[3]

For Rachel the competition lay in the fact that Leah was fertile and she was barren. Her older sister's sons surrounded her.

The depth of Rachel's emotion is evident in her cry to Jacob: "Give me children, or I'll die!" (Genesis 30:1).

Jacob responded, "Am I in the place of God, who has kept you from having children?" (Genesis 30:2).

Rachel began bringing her maidservants to Jacob's bed in order to have children through them. She even named one of those sons "Naphtali," which means "My struggle," and said, "I have had a great struggle with my sister, and I have won" (Genesis 30:8). The focus of Rachel's life seemed to be her competition with Leah. A scene between Rachel and Leah shows me the torture that these two women inflicted on each other.

Leah's son Reuben found some valuable mandrake plants during a wheat harvest. Mandrakes were thought to make a woman fertile. Rachel humbled herself and went to Leah, saying, "Please give me some of your son's mandrakes" (Genesis 30:14).

Leah, realizing she had the upper hand, let her bitterness spew: "Wasn't it enough that you took away my husband? Will you take my son's mandrakes too?" (Genesis 30:15).

Rachel knew that Leah longed to sleep with Jacob, so she told Leah that, in exchange for the mandrakes, she would allow Jacob to sleep with her that night. How humiliating!

But Leah grabbed the chance and cried out to God to help her have another son. God listened to her and gave her a fifth and a sixth son. As with Rachel, the focus of Leah's life seemed to be her competition with her sister.

It is not unusual for competition with a "wife-in-law" to be a strong undercurrent in a woman's life. That rivalry escalates when there are children involved—and the children are the victims caught in the middle.

The Children

Bitterness, unfortunately, is the norm between wives-in-law. One study of the children of divorce found that only 14 percent said that their mother and stepmother were on good terms. Forty-five percent said the feelings ran high and negative.[4]

Many first wives said it was hard for them to watch their ex-husband be a better father to his second set of children than he was to his first set. One woman told me, her green eyes flashing with anger, "Every year I remind both my ex and Sylvia that Kim's birthday is coming—but it doesn't do any good. He still forgets. It really rubs salt in Kim's wounds to see how attentive he is to the twins [his children by Sylvia]. As a teenager, Kim is acting out, I think, to get her dad's attention. She rolled her car last year and wound up in the hospital looking like she'd been beaten up by a gang. Could he come to see her? No—because the twins had Little League games every night that week. And I HATE Sylvia for not nudging him to be a decent father toward all his children."

Peace Despite Pain

Amazingly, despite the great pain, some wives-in-law have made peace with one another. The women I have known who have succeeded in this most difficult of relationships are women who have matured in their walk with Christ. Ann Cryster says that the inability to forgive and the inability to conquer the debilitating emotions of jealousy, resentment, and bitterness are the two most common obstacles preventing a healthy relationship between wives-in-law.

Lack of forgiveness, I've often heard described, is "the poison we drink hoping others will die." It is hard to forgive someone who has genuinely wronged you, especially if they are unrepentant. We cannot—absolutely cannot—do it on our own. But a prayer God is eager to answer is: *Lord, give me grace for _____. Give me genuine and not just outward forgiveness.* Professional biblical counseling can also be the lifeline when you are sinking in the quicksand of bitterness. We cannot get out by ourselves. We need the Spirit of God and His people to help us.

When you are a wife-in-law and there are children involved, you may be called upon to forgive again and again.

Leah struggled with resentment toward Rachel, in part, because of the favoritism Jacob showed toward Rachel's children. Jacob, a victim of parental favoritism and sibling rivalry himself, passed on this sin to his own children. He neglected Leah's children but lavished attention on Joseph, his son by Rachel, and later Benjamin, his other son by Rachel. Sibling rivalry ruled the home of Jacob.

> Now Israel [Jacob] loved Joseph more than any of his other sons, because he had been born to him in his old age; and he made a richly ornamented robe for him. When his brothers saw that their father loved him more than any of them, they hated him and could not speak a kind word to him. (Genesis 37:3–4)

I have wondered whether Jacob's favoritism and the resulting sibling rivalry might have been curbed had Rachel and Leah found a way, in the Lord, to become friends. They could have presented a united front to Jacob and perhaps spared their children their painful rivalry. Though it seems a tremendous task, I believe it would have been possible, with God's help. But the indications are strong that Rachel and Leah's religion was cultural rather than spiritual.

When Rachel left home, she stole her father's household gods. She hid them under her skirts and proclaimed her innocence. We may not have stone gods under our skirts, but sometimes we can cling to the gods of bitterness. *Forgive her? Forgive him? No way, but I'll pretend I have.*

What helps me to forgive when I have been truly hurt is to think about how much I've been forgiven. If Rachel had been a woman of faith, I believe she would have been able to forgive Leah for the part she played in Laban's deception. Instead, she held a grudge against Leah all of her life.

Jesus says that what comes out of our mouths reveals what is in our hearts, and there are streams of unpleasantness coming from Rachel's mouth. You can't really hide bitterness—it spills out, sooner or later.

When unforgiveness abounds, children often lose respect for their parents. In her book *Solomon's Children*, Glynnis Walker shares stories from adult children who viewed their parents' behavior as childish—and felt grieved that they were deprived of the joy that could have been theirs had their parents been able to behave maturely:

> They wouldn't attend the same family functions. Everyone had to phone around beforehand to make sure that so and so wasn't coming. If one showed up, the other left. My cousin's wedding was a fiasco. It made me very nervous about any sort of "family" occasion. So when I got married I didn't invite any of them, step-parents or parents, just some friends and my sister. I didn't want their stupidity to spoil my wedding.
>
> When my first child was born my mother and my stepmother both came to the hospital at the same time and went to the nursery to see the baby. My stepmother put her hand on my mother's arm to congratulate her. My mother reacted as if she had been touched by a leper and left the hospital building immediately. I felt sorry for my mother that she could be so hateful at such a joyous time. She missed so much she could have had.[5]

If a woman was able to behave in a reasonable fashion toward her wife-in-law, it impressed the children immeasurably. One young woman said: "They were great friends. My mother said she always liked Elaine and didn't blame her for anything. It made me respect my mother an awful lot for having such a mature attitude."[6]

Divorce is a minefield and you cannot walk through it without injury. Every wife-in-law has been genuinely hurt. It's hard to forgive. It's not natural to forgive. But it is possible to forgive through our resources in Christ.

The Godly Response of a Wife-in-Law

We can learn something of value from Leah's response to her pain. After giving birth to five sons, and each time hoping in vain that her husband would love her, she changed dreams. When she gave birth to her sixth son, she said: "This time my husband will treat me with honor, because I have borne him six sons" (Genesis 30:20). She was no longer hoping for love, just respect. Commentator Larry Richards says, "Life has meaning, even when hopes are unfulfilled."[7]

My friend Penny came to Christ after she married, but her husband did not. Eventually he had an affair and left her. For years, she clung to the dream that Matt would return to her and their little girl, Molly. She said, "Even when the dream was chipped away at—by evidences of Matt's contentment with Brooke [his new wife], with the birth of their baby, and with their move to another state—I still hoped.

"For years I clung unrealistically to the dream that Matt would come back. In so doing, I hurt Molly. I fed her hope of reconciliation. I did what I could to keep Molly from loving Brooke, because I was afraid if she did, it would be another nail in the coffin of my marriage to Matt.

"But as time went by, God helped me to see I was robbing Molly of the joy of childhood—and possibly maiming her for life. One year, when she was just six, after she had spent Christmas with Matt and Brooke, I found her in her room in tears. She told me she hated Christmas. A six-year-old? Hating Christmas?

"As I drew her out, I heard her parroting my criticisms of Brooke. God convicted me that Molly was reflecting my bitterness—and out of loyalty to me, was withholding her love and cooperation. We had a long talk that night, and I confessed to Molly that I had been wrong in not fully forgiving Brooke and her dad. That was a turning point. Her relationship with Matt and Brooke improved dramatically—and intriguingly, so did mine.

"I'm not sure Molly would be the godly young woman she is today if I had not grown up myself."

The first wife seems to find it easier to relinquish the dream of reconciliation if she remarries. (That's why so many second wives hope first wives will remarry!) But in Christ, a first wife can find peace without a husband. My friend Penny has—and other women have as well. Penny told me that she has found comfort in the story of Hagar.

"Hagar was a single mom like me. Abraham cast her out, along with his son Ishmael, at Sarah's request. In the desert Hagar and Ishmael are sobbing when an angel of God calls out to her and says: 'What is the matter, Hagar? Do not be afraid; God has heard the boy crying as he lies there' (Genesis 21:17). We are also told that God was with Ishmael as he grew up. This passage has been a great comfort to me—and I have definitely seen evidence that God has seen our tears and that He has been with Molly as she has grown up."

I am a new and relatively young widow, and I am just now understanding the enormous challenge of being alone and of parenting children—even adult children. How many times in this last year I have prayed, counting on His promises, "Lord, be my Husband! Help me get up this snowy driveway, hold me in the night, be my Protector, Provider, and Confidant."

I've also prayed, as a mother of three girls in their twenties, "Please be a Father to the fatherless—bring men into my daughters lives to stand in the gap." Time and time again I have seen Him bend down and answer this prayer. Within months after Steve's death, each daughter had a father figure. When we were having dinner on New Year's Eve with a former pastor, who now teaches preaching at Trinity Evangelical Seminary, he found out Sally was moving to Chicago and invited her to live with them. Sally and I looked at each other, tears welling up, recognizing

God's provision. When our daughter Beth moved to Kansas City, her big brother and sister-in-law fixed up an apartment in their basement for her. And then, our baby started dating our pastor's son, and found herself, week after week, at our pastor's dinner table, getting to know him more like a dad than a pastor.

We have a personal God who is not silent, who sees our pain, who hears our prayers. When we dwell on what we cannot have instead of embracing what we do have, we poison ourselves and the lives of those around us. Ann Cryster found through her interviews that many women dreamed of wrecking their wife-in-law's car, stealing her clothes, or spying on her in aerobics class. Relinquishing the dream of revenge may feel like a sacrifice, but it yields a harvest of righteousness that can come in no other way.

God cannot lead us down new paths if we have set our hearts on the old path. Our children are not likely to become godly individuals if their role models are harboring bitterness or dreams of revenge in their hearts. We reap what we sow. If we sow revenge, we will reap bitterness. If we sow love, we will reap joy. Ann makes a poignant plea:

> Will it really be such a bad thing if our daughter loves her stepmother? Will she really love us any less? In fact, what might make our kids appreciate us less is their sense of our compulsive competitiveness with their stepparents, because we tend at such times to be our worst selves.... It may feel like a frightening loss when our young daughter is delighted with her new step-mother, but, in fact, how can her added happiness detract from our own?[8]

The second wife also has pain to surmount and needs to draw upon her resources in Christ to do so. I spoke at a retreat in Los Angeles and stayed at the coordinator's home, who is a second wife. Kay's husband had come to Christ after his first marriage ended and then met and married Kay. For twenty years, Kay had been actively involved in the life of her stepdaughter, Lindy, though Lindy lived with her mother.

Kay said, "Lindy is as precious to me as my biological daughters—and she spent lots of time with us. God has blessed us with a rare and special relationship." But Kay's relationship with her "wife-in-law" has been strained as JoAnne has brought repeated lawsuits against her ex-husband to keep him from seeing Lindy and for more support. When Lindy married this spring, Kay had fears about the visit to Green Bay for the impending wedding. "And my worst nightmares came true," she said. "If it hadn't been for the restraint the Lord gave me, I might have taken an early plane back and ruined Lindy's day."

Kay's wife-in-law invited Kay, her husband, and the bride-to-be for a whitefish dinner two nights before the wedding. Kay said, "JoAnne had been to the hairdresser in the morning and then had been drinking all day. I expected that there would be other guests—but it was just us. JoAnne's inhibitions were overcome by the liquor and she began reminiscing about her wedding to my husband. It was very, very hard. I also could see that Lindy still had hopes, despite the fact that Chuck and I have been married for twenty years, that her parents would reconcile."

The rehearsal showed Kay that the wedding was going to have its share of pain for her. Kay said, with her eyes welling with tears, "Three times during the ceremony Lindy's mother was honored—but not me. I watched my husband standing up with his beautiful daughter on his arm and respond to the question, 'Who gives this woman …' with 'Her mother and I do.' I was a mother to Lindy too—but I was completely unrecognized. I felt like the unwelcome guest, the persona non grata.

"The reception line was difficult too. It's a strange feeling to have your husband standing between you and his ex. We greeted five hundred people and I felt God literally holding me up.

"But I am so thankful, looking back, for God's help. The morning of the wedding, I prayed that God would help me be gracious and to reflect Christ throughout the day. And though the sorrow was there, His grace prevailed. When everything was over, Lindy's grandmother handed me a note that Lindy had written. Alone in my room, I read her precious thank-you for the part I'd played in her life."

If you are like Kay and are living with pain (and who of us isn't?), your pain doesn't need to be wasted. God can bring beauty out of ashes if you learn from your pain and then pass on what you've learned to younger women. You don't have to be forty to be an older woman, for even at twenty you are older than someone. How different our lives would be if we would reach into our inexhaustible resources in Christ and help each other. We are sisters!

What can you do when a sister in Christ, when someone you love dearly, is on a path toward destruction? How can you restore her to her senses?

CAN AN EX-WIFE AND A NEW WIFE GET ALONG?

Reflections

Action Points

RESTORING OUR
SISTERS TO
THEIR SENSES

Then they can "train" the younger women (Titus 2:4). Train is the Greek word sophrorizo which means to restore to "soundness of mind" or to "one's senses."

—Strong's Exhaustive Concordance

CHAPTER 10

RESTORING OUR SISTERS TO THEIR SENSES

I love the description of the prodigal son just before he repents and returns to his loving father. Jesus says, "When he came to his senses …"

In the same way, the Bible tells "older" women to help "younger" women come to their senses! We have to be out of our minds to drift away from God! We have to have completely lost perspective to become like the foolish woman in Proverbs 14:1 who "tears down her own house with her own hands." For this reason God makes it very clear that we need to help each other by restoring each other to our senses! But how?

First, we must be immersed in God's Word—for only then can we overcome our own deceitful hearts. Then we must be sensitive to His Spirit and to every person He brings across our path.

Bringing Women to Christ

When my older sister Sally was teaching Spanish at a college in Ames, Iowa, she told her class, "Write a one-page essay in Spanish, explaining who your best friend is—and why."

A freshman named Bonnie wrote about Jesus! Clearly she said that Jesus was her very best friend because He had paid for her

sin and reconciled her to God. My sister was intrigued and pur-
sued the subject with Bonnie. Bonnie was scared, but she also
was confident that she belonged to a BIG GOD who could do
wonderful things in her teacher's life. And He did!

Likewise, my sister Sally believed that she belonged to a BIG
GOD who could do wonderful things in the lives of others. Sally
was very sensitive to the leading of His Holy Spirit each day.
When my sister had her time with God, she would say: "I have
given You my life. Impress on my heart how You want me to
spend this day." And God began impressing on her heart that she
should visit me, lift up the claims of Christ, and allow Him to
bring me to my senses! My sister obeyed, God reconciled me
(and my husband!) to Himself, and now He has given me, as He
has each of His children, a ministry of reconciliation.

My first opportunity came with my neighbor, Carol. Carol
and I had a deep friendship, as women do, and so it was a natural opportunity for me. We had many theological discussions.
One question she had was: "Why should I worship Jesus? Why
not Buddha? Or Confucius?"

Fresh from reading C. S. Lewis's *Mere Christianity*, I said:

> Buddha and Confucius did not claim to be God. Man
> has chosen to worship them, but they did not ask for
> worship. Jesus did. Jesus claimed to be God! Jesus was
> very different from all religious leaders. Instead of say-
> ing: 'Here is the way, follow it,' He said, 'I am the way
> and the truth and the life. No one comes to the Father
> except by me' (John 14:6). C. S. Lewis says that each of
> us needs to decide whether Jesus was a liar, a lunatic, or
> telling the truth. Either we should spit in His face or fall
> on our knees and worship Him.

Carol was pensive.

"Carol, why don't you ask God to show you the truth?"

"Okay, I will!" She went home and said, "Show me if Jesus
alone is to be worshipped, God." Then she flipped open her

Bible, pointed her finger, and landed on Mark 9. Here Peter, James, and John are at the Transfiguration and are ready to worship Jesus—but also Moses and Elijah! God's voice booms from heaven to set them straight. "This is My Son, whom I love. Listen to Him!" Suddenly, when they looked around, they no longer saw anyone with them except Jesus. Carol understood the message and came running down to my house to tell me. I hugged her and said, "Well—will you receive Christ now?"

"Not yet," she said.

A few months later Carol thought she was miscarrying. "God," she cried, "if You just let me keep this baby, I will give my life to Jesus!"

God let her keep the baby, and she backed out of the deal. (She did give fifty dollars to a poverty-relief organization!) I was discouraged—and when we moved away from Indianapolis it was tempting to give up on the friendship. Yet God's Spirit didn't let me! There was so much about Carol that I valued: her zest, her smile, and her capable mind. We kept in touch at Christmas and exchanged an occasional letter. Twenty years later I was speaking in Indianapolis and called her, hoping for a lunch date. "I can't," she said, her voice breaking.

"Carol?"

"Bob has a brain tumor, Dee. My husband is barely forty, but he's dying. I cannot leave his side." Together, on the phone, we cried.

A year later, after Bob had died, I was back in Indianapolis. This time Carol met me for breakfast. "I heard you on 'Focus on the Family,'" she said quietly.

"Carol, are you listening to Christian radio?"

"You can't go through what I've just been through without God. Dee, tell me about Jesus again."

Carol received Christ and has even made some inquiries into full-time Christian ministry. A few months ago she married a Christian man. The words God led me to say over twenty years ago eventually brought my friend to her senses!

I am convinced that there are many people that God brings across our path who would be open to spiritual things—if we would just seize the opportunity. The late Paul Little said once, "I have never known of anyone whom the Lord has used mightily in personal evangelism who did not have a sensitivity to the people God brought across his or her path."[1]

Often those who are most passionate about bringing others to Christ are new Christians. When I was a new Christian, I practically stopped people in the grocery store. I left tracts everywhere. I was constantly aware of the fact that they might be headed toward eternity without a Savior. But as the years went by, I lost that zeal. I transferred some of it toward social issues, like abortion and pornography. And while I believe those are important, and that part of being salt and light means trying to slow down the decadence in our world, God has reminded me that my most important mission is to bring others to Him.

God has used a friend to renew my vision. Marilyn Pendleton, a winsome young mother of three with a 600-watt smile, has a very aggressive form of cancer, and her doctors give her little hope. But her attitude is amazing. She wrote to me, saying, "Two years ago I realized I'd lost my passion, my first love, and I told God to do whatever it took to restore it. Although many have viewed this as a tragedy, it has been a gift. Not many people get a picture of their own mortality at age thirty-six. God has given me a new urgency, a new boldness, about sharing Christ."

Marilyn has caused me to search my own heart: Have I lost my first love? My urgency? My boldness for sharing Christ?

I also need to ask myself if there are times when I avoid confronting my friends because I fear they will withdraw from me. As a woman I have such a strong drive for connection that it would be easy to avoid confrontation, even when I see them heading toward a precipice. And I am most reluctant with my closest friends—the very friends who would probably be the most open to my words! But what would Jesus do? He would speak the truth in love to them and try to restore them to their senses!

God may very well bring a woman across your path who is headed toward disaster: an abortion, marriage to an unbeliever, an affair.... God has shown me that one of the most effective ways to "restore a friend to her senses" is to gently help her to see what the consequences of her choice will be.

The Soft Approach: Helping Her See the Consequences

"I can't even remember the last time Mike and I were intimate—that's how long it's been."

Amy's mug of coffee sat untouched, growing cold as she twisted her single blonde braid, tearfully explaining the state of her sixteen-year marriage. "There's so much anger—we go to bed in icy silence. The only time we talk is when we exchange sarcastic barbs. Can you understand, Dee? I've got to get out of this marriage!" She searched my eyes for compassion.

I looked down. I knew Mike was a good man. Somehow Amy and Mike had gotten themselves into a downward spiral, but this wasn't a marriage that should end. I was afraid sympathy would push Amy over the divorce cliff, so I was quiet, trying to decide how to respond. The room was still.

My reserve infuriated Amy. She stood abruptly, grabbed her camel jacket from the back of the chair, and said, "You don't understand! How easy it is for a happily married person to be self-righteous about divorce! Dee, you just don't know what it's like to live with a man you don't love anymore. Mike never compliments me, never touches me.... Oh, never mind!"

Amy turned and headed for the door. I quickly followed, "Amy," I pleaded, catching her arm.

Jerking it away, she reached for the door: "I don't know why I came to you. I guess I was stupid enough to think that after eight years of friendship you might care about my pain." Sobbing, Amy ran to her car and screeched up the driveway.

Turning back into my house, I refuted her last accusation. I did care! I thought back to the night our friendship with Amy and Mike cemented. It had been Christmastime, and they and their three tow-headed tots had come caroling, offering a plate of fresh-from-the-oven sugar cookies: stars, bells, and snowmen dusted with sprinkles. We'd invited them in and talked and laughed for over an hour. Before they left I asked for an encore of "O Come All Ye Faithful" so I could take their picture. I pulled out the album and found it. How happy they looked! How could this family be ending? How could I make Amy think rationally?

The photo in my hand reminded me of a comment my friend Beth had made. Darkly attractive, with a rare mix of sophistication and warmth, Beth and her husband, Dave, had made a unique contribution to our adult Sunday school class. Both had been married before and vulnerably admit that leaving their first loves was a mistake, even though they are determined to make their marriage to each other work.

I remember the day Beth stilled the class with her candor: "There's a million reasons not to leave your first love—right down to the little things—like photo albums! Who gets them? And who wants them? Because looking at your once-whole, happy family is extremely painful."

I wondered if there was any chance that Amy might agree to meet with Beth. She'd been so angry when she left. If I called, would she cut me off, assuming I was getting ready to give her a sermon? How could I gain a hearing?

Breaking Down the Barrier

I called Beth, explaining the situation with Amy and Mike. I told her that, though they were faithful church attendees, their church didn't emphasize personal faith or the Scriptures—so I wasn't sure how responsive she'd be to a scriptural approach.

Beth said: "I've found that even people who know Christ are not responsive to Scripture at this point. Often they've hardened their hearts because they feel God's way is too painful. The only thing that might work is to show them that divorce will be more painful. Amy needs to see what her life will be like if she divorces Mike. I'd be happy to meet with her!"

I so appreciated Beth's willingness—but I wondered, *Would Amy come?*

Sensing my thoughts, Beth said, "Dee, the fact that Amy came to you is a very hopeful sign. Let's bathe this situation in prayer. Then make a casserole, go over, and see if she's receptive."

Armed with lasagna, I rang Amy's doorbell. When she opened the door and saw me, she softened. She took the pan from me and gestured for me to follow her into the kitchen. Placing it on the counter, she tuned toward me tearfully and we embraced.

"I do care about you, Amy." I sobbed.

"I know," she said, gasping.

I told her about Beth, and then I said, "I promise—no pressure. I just thought talking to Beth would give you a better idea of what your life will be like if you divorce Mike."

Amy was quiet. Then she said, "I guess it couldn't hurt."

Considering the Consequences

We began talking while the October sun shone warmly through the window—and kept talking until it had sunk behind the golden trees on the hill across the lake.

Beth began, her voice intent. "I know you think, Amy, that it couldn't get any worse than it is. That divorce has to be better. But very, very seldom does that turn out to be true. I'm absolutely convinced that God never intended us to leave our first loves, the spouse with whom we shared so many firsts: your children's births; Johnny's first steps; Mary's first dance when she floated down the steps into the living room; your first home; even those struggling first years when you existed on macaroni and cheese."

"Why did you leave your first love, Beth?" I asked while Amy listened silently, her cool hands finding comfort around the steaming mug of coffee.

Beth answered carefully: "Because I was deceived by my own heart—with a little help by the values all around me. I felt like life was passing me by. I began to be irritated by all kinds of little things about my husband. He was too skinny. I thought he had ugly fingers. He was a farmer and sometimes he had dirt in his ears. I know it sounds ridiculous, but at the time I felt that if there was going to be any hope for happiness for me, I had to leave.

"A few years after the divorce, though, I thought, *What was the matter with me? He was a good man!* During that time of brokenness I came to Christ. But though He made me a new creation, and filled the emptiness in me, that doesn't mean I escaped the consequences of my sinful choice."

I got up and filled our coffee cups. "Tell us about those consequences," I prodded.

"It's hard to know where to start. There are big things, of course, but almost harder are the daily little tensions. Like how you'll feel at your child's basketball game as he looks longingly back and forth between you and your ex, who has carefully placed himself on the opposite end of the bleachers.

"There's the endless tension about money. Even now with our kids grown, who pays for schoolbooks, graduation expenses, the wedding reception? You may think things are tight now—but you'll probably become one of America's new poverty class: the single mother. Ask around, Amy, and see how divorcees are living.

"But the worst pain is that we've permanently damaged our children. We let them down. Their role models betrayed their trust and they are in search of different role models. Their chances of a happy marriage have been drastically reduced—the statistics verify that. And we feel a lack of respect. Sometimes they openly verbalize it. It hurts, Amy."

Beth took out a tissue and blew her nose loudly. We laughed, relieving our tension. I said, "I think it's time for food!" We laughed again, glad for a momentary diversion. I brought out cheese, apples, and knives. I put a bowl of freshly toasted pumpkin seeds on the table.

Reaching for a handful of seeds, Beth said, reflectively, "Family traditions, like carving pumpkins and putting up the Christmas tree, are changed. The kids are always thinking of the missing parent. We all dread the holidays. The kids aren't eager to be with me or my ex-husband.

"They aren't particularly comfortable with our new spouses. Home isn't home. There's constant friction concerning where they'll go, and when they come it's painful—because it isn't the same for them. It isn't the same for me either. I can't turn to David and say, 'Do you remember the Christmas when Johnny ...' because David wasn't there. And special occasions, like birthdays, graduations, weddings, etc., are all filled with distress. The pain won't quit—and often, it's terribly intense."

"How old were your children when you left?" Amy asked.

Beth smiled, seeming to read her thoughts. "Only one was still in the nest—and she was in her senior year so she stayed with my husband. Lots of people will tell you that once the kids are out of the nest, it's OK to leave, but I'll tell you, Amy, it's not so. My oldest daughter, who was twenty-four, suffered the most.

"I repeat: We've permanently damaged our children. Their self-esteem. Their security. Their memories. Their future. And, even though they are grown now, the pain continues. Our relationship with our grandchildren, for example, is extremely complicated. They've got so many grandparents, they're not even sure what to call us all!"

Beth shook her head sadly: "Humpty Dumpty cannot be put back together again—at least not in this world. The sins of the fathers, and the mothers, are visited on the next generation, and the next, and the next."

Amy was silent. Thoughtful. Beth interrupted her pensiveness with a question. "Amy, have you told the children what you're considering?"

Twisting her braid, Amy responded, "I've talked to the two older ones. I wanted to know, if they had a choice, with whom they would live. Our son said he didn't know. And our daughter said she would leave it up to the judge because she didn't want to hurt either of our feelings. I'd been so confident they'd both choose me. Now I'm not sure."

"It puts them in a terrible position," Beth responded. "And they'll hate you for doing it to them. I have another question, Amy. It's none of my business, but I'm going to ask anyhow. Is there someone else?"

I was shocked to see Amy nod. But Beth seemed to expect it.

Amy glanced at me and said, "There's been nothing physical but there's a man at work who makes me feel good about myself in a way that Mike hasn't for a long, long time."

"Satan knows when to attack," Beth said. "Amy, you have to separate yourself from this man. Satan is waiting at the door, longing to overpower you. He seeks to destroy you and your family." Beth continued, "If you divorce Mike, how will you feel when he finds someone else?"

Amy said, "I've been telling myself no one else would want him."

"Amy!" I interrupted. "Mike is kind and hardworking! Beth, let me show you his picture." I got out the album and started looking.

As I turned pages, Beth said, "Even if he's homely, Amy, women will flock around him. He'll be remarried within two years. Count on it. And chances are, he'll marry a divorcee with kids. Kids with whom your kids will have to share their dad and their lives."

I showed Beth the picture of the family, singing a carol on our front porch. Mike, a good-looking, muscular man, had his arm around Amy, his blue eyes full of joy.

"Wow," Beth said, shaking her head.

Amy took the picture from Beth, looking at Mike as if with new eyes. She admitted, "When I think of Mike with someone else, I realize I still have some feelings. I've felt like if the divorce didn't work, I could have Mike back. But maybe not."

At this encouragement, Beth leaned over and put her hand on Amy's. "I'm convinced it's possible to restore the feelings you and Mike had for each other in the beginning. If you start, Amy, I'm confident you have the power to release Mike's love for you. Men long for respect from their wives. When Mike feels that again, you'll see a change in his attitude toward you. I've counseled other women who felt like you did—and I've seen them, because of a change of attitude, and with help from God, turn their marriage back to what it was in the beginning."

Amy turned a corner that day. She left with a different perspective. That night she fixed Mike's favorite supper: stuffed pork chops. She put candles on the table. The next day when Amy told me about it, she seemed lighter, freer. She laughed when she told me, "Mike walked in the door, saw the candles, and said, angrily: 'Who's coming for dinner?' He looked so surprised when I told him it was just for him and the kids."

Amy took another important step when she confronted the man at work who'd been unusually attentive toward her. She called Beth and said, "I told him some of the things you told me. And I told him, in no uncertain terms, that I was recommitting myself to my marriage. He's backed off gracefully."

My friend Beth taught me a lot through her example about how to bring younger women "to their senses." The hard-line approach of shooting Scripture at them often backfires, but if you can help them to see that the consequences of their choice could be very painful, you may gain a listening ear.

Recently I was involved in "crisis intervention" for a friend who suffers from an eating disorder. She needed help but no one had been successful in persuading her to get help. Success came when several of us banded together! We contacted the Minirth-Meier Clinic and they suggested working with Keith Hankinson, a man skilled in interventions.[2] We met with Keith in a hotel room for an afternoon. After a time of prayer, we each composed letters telling our friend why we loved her, a behavior we had seen that concerned us, and a plea to her to get help immediately.

Then, together, we went to her, read her our letters, and persuaded her to go with Mr. Hankinson that day and admit herself to the Minirth-Meier Clinic. She is on the road to recovery now! Mr. Hankinson told me that modern interventions are based on Matthew 18:15–17. "Some people think," he said, "that if a person doesn't want help that there is nothing you can do. That's simply not true." Mr. Hankinson works primarily with addictions (alcohol, drugs, gambling), eating disorders, and mental illness. But surely this approach could be used by a group of caring women when they see their "sister" headed toward any kind of disaster.

We Are Sisters

Surely part of the high calling of being sisters in Christ is to speak the truth in love to each other. And yet, I've found it is the exception, even for close sisters in Christ, to be in the *habit* of taking one another higher.

Maybe it is because they are Italian, and outspoken, but I've watched with admiration as Kathy Troccoli and one of her best friends, Ellie Lofaro, continually point out one another's blind spots and receive one another with teachable spirits. Yet if we agree with Scripture that our depravity is real, then whether we are an outspoken Italian or a reserved Anglo-Saxon, we should stretch toward honesty in our communication with one another. Not only should we speak the truth, we absolutely must receive it with humble hearts.

I respect the friends who are *willing to risk relationship with me to speak the truth.* Though it smarted when Shirley told me, as a young mom, "You've just got to follow through better with disciplining your boys, Dee. If you do not, you will ruin their lives."

I am so thankful when Kathy Troccoli tells me that I am not loving someone well—and why. The friends I go to when I need the truth are the friends who will put my relationship with Christ over their relationship with me.

Recently, for example, I went to Allyson—because I know I can trust her to tell me the truth. I had a friend who was asking a lot of me—and I wondered if I was simply lacking in compassion. Allyson said, "You've enabled her. You've helped her too much in the past and now she expects it from you. Dee, you must go to her and repent." Allyson always begins with my repentance, but I love her for it. Very seldom is the sin on just one side.

I also appreciate so much my friends who have teachable hearts—who will listen with hearing ears if I do talk to them, and not immediately become defensive. My dear friend Jill, who is as pure a heart as I know, will get tears in her eyes and say, "What you say, Dee, is true and I receive it. Thank you for speaking the truth to me." This is why Jill keeps going higher. Like the Shulamite maiden, she is willing to die to self to go higher, saying, "I will go to the mountain of myrrh" (Song of Songs 4:6). Jill, and those with teachable hearts, are miles above those who become defensive, proud, and resistant.

How we need honesty in the body of Christ. We are sisters and we must speak the truth to one another. Sometimes that is the truth of confrontation, other times it is the truth of saying, "I am hurting; I am carrying an overburden. Please help me." Too often our pride makes us like the mountain climber who is hanging to a precipice by his fingernails, but when asked if he needs help, says, "I'm just fine."

Have you ever been hesitant to ask for help?

RESTORING OUR SISTERS TO THEIR SENSES

Reflections

Action Points

SISTERS: WALKING THE ROAD TOGETHER

CHAPTER 11

SISTERS: WALKING THE ROAD TOGETHER

"I can't be sick, Lord!"

Nauseated, I fell back on the pillow and continued pleading, "Please, Lord—not with two ever-present toddlers!"

I pulled my legs into a fetal position and waited for instant healing.

"Plan B. Please, Lord, if I have to be sick, at least let the boys sleep in this morning."

No sooner had I uttered my prayer than I heard the squeak of the crib rail from the nursery and the soft thump of little feet, clad in Winnie-the-Pooh pajama sleepers, hitting the floor. I shut my eyes against the inevitable. The bedroom door burst open. The smell of a soggy diaper filled the air as Johnny stood beside my bed, watching me. Discerning my sleep was feigned, he said, "Mommy, I'm hungry."

"Mommy's sick, sweetheart. Do you think you could find the Pop Tarts in the cupboard? And could you bring me a diaper?"

He padded quickly away. I hoped his assignment would take a long, long time.

But in two minutes he was back, Pop Tart in hand. Dropping crumbs, Johnny crawled first on the bed, then on me. Small, sticky fingers pried open my eyelids. "Are you better yet, Mommy?"

I considered calling Patti. I knew she would take the boys, but I didn't want to impose. Patti was important to me—what if my request strained our friendship? I didn't call.

Before that incredibly long day was over, J. R., our firstborn, downed a whole bottle of orange-flavored children's aspirin as his inattentive mother dozed on the couch. We emptied his stomach and he survived, but I began to see my foolishness in not calling Patti.

That day occurred thirty-five years ago and those toddlers are now men. Our three daughters are grown as well, so when I get sick, I sleep in uninterrupted bliss. But if I really need help, I've learned to ask.

Asking for help, rather than being a sign of weakness, is a sign of strength because it demonstrates humility, the recognition that there are times in my life when I need help to carry an over-burden. And if the need is genuine, rather than straining a friendship, asking for help cements it.

Cementing a Friendship

Early on in my friendship with Shell, I found myself in need again. I was scheduled to speak at a luncheon in Lincoln. The only child we had at home at that time was Sally. My plan was to drop her at school and then get on I-80 and head for my speaking engagement. On the way to school, however, Sally vomited in the front seat. We made a hasty retreat for home, where I cleaned up my daughter, put her in bed, and went back to clean up the car and, finally, myself. With time getting short, I was frantically trying to come up with solutions. As I cleaned, I thought of three options:

1) I could call and cancel. ("But how can I, Lord? They're expecting three hundred women! They've been planning for months!")
2) I could take Sally with me and have her lie down in the coat room. (I pictured my little waif huddled behind the coats with a bucket while I spoke about being a good mother.)

3) I could call Shell, who was my closest friend in this new town, and ask for help. ("But isn't this a lot to ask, Lord? Is our friendship too young?")

The third option, though frightening to me, seemed the best. Hesitantly, I picked up the phone. I explained my dilemma to Shell—and then I gave her room to wiggle out if she felt imposed upon. I said, "If you have something else going on today, that's fine, because I have other options." And then I prayed and held my breath, hoping I wouldn't have to use one of those other very undesirable options.

Without hesitation, Shell said: "Bring her right over. I insist. I'm getting a bed ready."

Shell's enthusiastic response lifted the burden from my shoulders. Had she said, "Well, if you can't find someone else ..." I would have retreated. I might even have felt "let down," despite the fact I had minimized my need. How I pray that I can be as intuitive and flexible as Shell was when a woman comes to me and drops clues about a deep need!

Sally brightened to see the room Shell had prepared. Blue flowered pillows had been fluffed against the headboard of the bed. A stack of comic books, a handheld video game, and a tall glass of 7-Up sat on the bedside table.

No longer reluctant to have me leave, Sally hugged me good-bye. Feeling considerably lighter, I walked down the stairs with Shell. Before I left, we paused for a moment to pray. It touched me deeply when Shell said with emotion, "Thank You so much, dear Lord, that Dee trusted me enough to come to me with her need."

When a friend responds to your need, at great sacrifice, it cements the friendship. I have known and admired author and speaker Liz Curtis Higgs only in passing—as a gifted, side-splittingly funny, and increasingly pithy speaker. When she heard Steve might be dying, she started e-mailing me. Soon she was on my e-mail prayer list and was often the first to respond with empathy, prayer, and love.

When it was clear Steve *was* dying, and I had retreats I simply couldn't do, Liz was willing to break her precious sabbatical. She said, "I'll go at the drop of a hat, Dee. And I'll send the honorarium to you." How could I *not* love a woman like that? That kind of response *cements* a friendship.

Hearing the Unspoken Request

I have found linguist Deborah Tannen's observations about the way women make requests fascinating. Tannen says we are much less direct than men because we are more concerned about "breaking connections." Rather than saying, "Could you take care of Tommy tomorrow while I go to the dentist?" many women will instead hint, saying, "I don't know what to do with Tommy while I'm at the dentist tomorrow."

Now any dodo bird should know she's asking for help with Tommy, but she doesn't dare to be direct. This teaches me to read between the lines when a soul mate shares a need with me—and to respond enthusiastically with an offer to help.

A woman named Julie Hines wrote me a particularly moving story of a time in her life when she desperately needed her friend Suzanne—but was afraid to ask.

Julie wrote, "When my husband and I were overseas, we faced the greatest crisis of our lives when our baby was born with spina bifida. Even though my husband was wonderful, I needed a woman friend to help carry my pain. I needed Suzanne. Without my having to ask, because I couldn't ask for so much, she moved a little of heaven and earth to fly over. I will never forget our greeting scene in the Bologna airport. It felt like a physical lightening of my load."

Go to God First

Many times in my walk as a Christian wife and mother, I've needed advice. It's not nearly as hard to ask for advice as it is for other kinds of help. Perhaps as a result, often my first response when

I'm troubled is to pick up the phone and call an empathetic friend. But God has been teaching me that a woman who is mature will run first to Him. Until I have been still before Him, until I have sought the Scriptures for His wisdom, it's too soon to run to a friend.

When we were living in Seattle, I was trying to teach our new Springer spaniel puppy, Darling, to stay within the boundaries of our yard without a fence. While reading on our back porch one autumn afternoon, I heard the angry cries of my neighbor. "GET OUT! SCAT! YOU $#+&# DOG!!!!!!" I looked up, alarmed, to see Darling digging in her rhododendrons.

I ran over, scooped up our puppy, and said, "I'm so sorry!"

My neighbor stormed into her house, slamming the door behind her. I retreated up our path with Darling. I asked myself, "What could I do to smooth this over?" My husband often had received fish from his patients. So I went to our freezer, took out a salmon, and headed back to my neighbor's. When she opened the door, I said, "Would you take this salmon as a peace offering?"

She surprised me by saying: "Fish! I've got a freezer full of fish! That's the last thing I need." Then she closed the door in my face.

Embarrassed, I retreated again. In the safety of my house, I curled up in an overstuffed chair and nursed my wounds, telling the Lord that I had tried. After all, Darling was just a puppy— wasn't my neighbor partly to blame for being so intolerant? And I had apologized—wasn't my neighbor now the one who was in the wrong? Wasn't the ball in her court?

My first response was to call a friend whom I knew would empathize with me—who would tell me how honorably I'd behaved and what a rat my neighbor was. I called Patti—no answer. Beth—her line was busy. Lorinda—nobody home. Beth— still busy.

Forced to go to the Friend who wasn't busy and was at home, I sat down and prayed again: "Lord, what should I do now?"

Instead of comforting me, He brought Romans 12:18 to mind: "If it is possible, as far as it depends on you, live at peace with everyone."

It seemed the Lord was nudging me to try again! Reluctantly,

I looked around. Our flowers were past their bloom. Our cookie jar, empty.

"Lord," I said, "I don't have anything to give her!"

I am convinced that our Lord has a great sense of humor, for at that moment, the UPS truck pulled up in front. The man carried a crate of beautiful Florida oranges and grapefruit to our door—a gift from my mother-in-law. Moments later I was headed back to my neighbor's with a cardboard tray of citrus fruit.

After ringing the doorbell, I stood there, nervously. This time, when she opened the door, she was the astonished one. After a long silence, she broke into a grin. "You don't give up, do you, honey?" She took the fruit and walked away, shaking her head and chuckling.

I learned so much from this experience, for my relationship with that neighbor was warm and good from that moment on. Whereas she hadn't been particularly friendly before, now she smiled and waved when I drove into the driveway. If I had been successful in reaching a friend when I needed advice, she probably would have sympathized with me, telling me I had tried hard enough. That's not to say that friends always give poor advice, but simply to say that the very best advice, the advice that can never be wrong, is from the Lord.

If you've gone to the Lord and He seems silent and the way seems unclear, I believe it's appropriate to go to a woman friend. But go to the godliest women you know—particularly women who have been where you are going and have done it well.

When I originally wrote *We Are Sisters,* I faced one of the hardest decisions of my life. How I pleaded with the Lord for His counsel. He in turn impressed on my heart to go and talk to the godliest women I knew. Then He worked through my sisters in an amazing way. When I reflect back on that time I am still overcome with awe.

The Crisis

At the age of forty-five, I was the mother of four children and also had a busy writing and speaking career. The empty nest loomed ahead, but the thought of having more children didn't even occur to me. The next logical step seemed to be grandchildren!

One day I was unloading the dishwasher when Steve walked in the kitchen and announced: "Honey—I've been thinking about it, and I think we should adopt another special-needs child: an older child, or a handicapped child, or a sibling group."

I practically dropped the china plate I was holding. I said: "I don't think so. I don't see how I could possibly handle that. I think we should just pray we'll soon be grandparents!"

"Well," Steve responded, "would you be willing to pray about it?"

"Sure, honey. I'll pray about it."

"I mean—let's pray about it right now," Steve persisted. "Let's go into the living room and ask God to impress His desires on our hearts. And, honey ..."

"Yes?"

"I will try to get rid of my overwhelming desire to adopt a child if you will try to get rid of your resistance."

"Okay," I replied weakly.

We knelt down and were quiet for the longest time. No overwhelming desire came into my heart to adopt a special-needs child or children. No Scripture verses about caring for the fatherless came into my head. Finally I looked up to see my husband overcome with emotion. He said: "I just heard a little girl—and she was crying. She's older ..."

I said, "I think you imagined this."

He said, "I might have. Let's just see if God confirms this in another way."

Three days passed in which I could think about little else. I knew that God was up to something! (Recently I listened to a humorous but insightful tape from a charismatic preacher named Ed Silvoso. He was telling charismatic Christians how to be culturally sensitive when talking to evangelical Christians. He said, "Don't say, 'God spoke to me,' but instead say, 'God gave me an insight,' because God doesn't speak to evangelicals, He writes to them." I laughed! However, in this case, God spoke to an evangelical! I admit, however, it is unusual! Maybe that's what made me so apprehensive.)

Then, as I suspected might happen, God's voice was confirmed. Barbara Kim, a social worker with Holt,[1] a Christian adoption agency, called me. We had worked with Barbara when we adopted our youngest daughter, Anne. Barbara said:

> Dee, we've just been to an orphanage in Thailand where we met a little girl who stole our hearts. She's almost ten—and all that is wrong with her is that she's missing her left arm. It was amputated and she was abandoned. But she's beautiful—and has a spirit that reminded us of your daughter Sally. She'd be between the ages of Sally and Annie. We thought you might consider adopting her. Could I send you her picture?

I'll never forget the day Steve opened the envelope and Beth's picture fell out. With tears in his eyes he said: "This is our little girl." Then he looked at me, saw that I was trembling, and said: "But we won't do this, honey, unless you feel you can."

I felt like God was asking me to sail into a storm! Like a rowboat on the high seas, I tossed about, wanting to be supportive of my husband, but overcome with fears. I had prayed, but the way seemed dark and cloudy. At that point it seemed wise to seek godly counsel so I sought out spiritually mature women who would do their best to help me discern God's will.

Shell Ramey: Earnest Counsel

Shell listened to me intently, the way I knew she would. She prayed with me—and then she went home. She spent the whole day in prayer and in Scripture. Then she wrote me a ten-page letter. First she wrote out many Scriptures that she thought might be helpful to me—Scriptures like the following:

Religion that God our Father accepts as pure and fault-
less is this: to look after orphans and widows in their
distress. (James 1:27)

Wives, submit to your husbands as to the Lord. For
the husband is the head of the wife as Christ is the head
of the church, his body, of which he is the Savior. Now as
the church submits to Christ, so also wives should submit
to their husbands in everything. (Ephesians 5:22–24)

Then, to soften the blow of the Scriptures, she wrote me a
beautiful, loving letter, telling me that it seemed to her that the
Lord was leading us to do this, but that if I didn't receive His
peace, that she didn't think I should go ahead. Either way, she
would stand by my side. Shell's earnest response reminded me of
Proverbs 27:9: "Perfume and incense bring joy to the heart, and
the pleasantness of one's friend springs from his earnest counsel."

Jean Hueser: Praying with Me for Wisdom

I walk with my friend Jean regularly, and it is our habit to walk
and talk, then walk and pray. During this time of indecision, Jean
prayed with me every day, pleading with God for His guidance.
One prayer of Jean's, which I remember, was, "Lord, please put
Your desires in Dee's heart. Give her Your peace if this is of You."

Sara Andreesen: Drawing Out the
Deep Waters of My Soul

Solomon says, "The purposes of a man's heart are deep waters,
but a man of understanding draws them out" (Proverbs 20:5). So,
over taco salads at a restaurant appropriately called Amigos, Sara
drew me out. This was our conversation, as I recall it.

"Dee," Sara began, "let's try to figure out why you are afraid.
Are you afraid because this girl is almost ten? Are you afraid it's
too late to mold her?"

"A little," I responded. "Many children don't survive being raised in an institution—they are emotionally maimed and can't seem to recover. But the social workers seem so confident that she's a survivor. And, I wouldn't want a baby—or even a toddler. In fact, I like it that she's close in age to Annie. Perhaps God has this planned, in part, for Annie."

"Well, then," Sara continued. "Let's see. Are you afraid of her handicap? Are you afraid there are many things she won't be able to do and that you will constantly be helping her?"

"I don't think so," I answered. "Steve works with amputees a lot, and he thinks that since she's been without her arm all her life, that there's very little she won't be able to do." I paused, emotion rising in me.

"Go on," Sara encouraged.

"He says she will probably do some things with her teeth and her feet."

"And how do you feel about that?" Sara prodded.

Now my tears were flowing. "I don't want her to do things with her teeth and her feet."

Sara sipped her Coke. She had drawn out the deep waters of my soul. What we found wasn't very pretty: I was worried about appearances! Then she reached over and clasped my hand, laughing softly, empathetically. "You are mature in so many ways, Dee," she began gently, "but maybe this is an area where God is asking you to grow."

Solomon says, "Wounds from a friend can be trusted" (Proverbs 27:6).

Janet Yost: An Offer to Stand by My Side and Help

Finally, I went to my friend Janet. Janet is a godly older woman— she is where I want to be in ten years. She is so patient and loving as she ministers to those in need, particularly those from other countries who are lonely, poor, and struggling to learn English.

Like my other friends, Janet told me that she felt I should have God's peace before I went ahead. But then she said, "If you do this, Dee, I will stand by your side and help you. You can bring your daughter to my house for an hour every day, and I will help her to learn English."

The writer of Ecclesiastes says, "Two are better than one, because they have a good return for their work: If one falls down, his friend can help him up. But pity the man who falls and has no one to help him up!" (Ecclesiastes 4:9–10).

The cumulative effect of my multitude of counselors was that God filled me with His peace, the sign for which everyone had been praying!

Walking the Rocky Road of Faith Together

Often, when God leads you in an adventure of faith, the road is not easy! Our first surprise was that it took us three years to get Beth! (I don't want to discourage those of you thinking of overseas adoptions. With countries like Korea, Vietnam, and China the time is usually shorter than a pregnancy. But Thailand was mired in red tape.) I didn't take any speaking engagements for two years—so that I could get off on the right foot as a mother. But, as so often happens, God's timing is different from ours. Those years came and went and we didn't have Beth.

The third year, my calendar was booked with retreats! There was only one time when I could see that I would be free to fly to Thailand for the two required weeks. From February 14 to the twenty-eighth, I was free. Therefore, in January, I began praying in earnest that Holt would call. And they did! But instead of asking us to fly out on February 14, they asked us to go on February 1!

My heart sank as I looked at my calendar. I had retreats in California, Kansas, and Rhode Island in those first two weeks. My thoughts were anything but tranquil. "What are You doing, Lord? What kind of a mother doesn't pick up the child she's adopting?" And, with a heavy heart, I made plane reservations for my husband and my daughter Sally, who would go in my place on February 1.

However, again, my sisters in Christ came through. They prayed an amazing prayer of faith. They prayed that the authorities in Thailand would change their mind and back up the date by two weeks. I shook my head in disbelief. *No way,* I thought. *Dream on.*

Beth in Thailand

Yet shortly before Steve and Sally were to leave without me, Cheri, a worker from Holt, called and said, "We're sorry to tell you this, but your trip has been postponed until February 14." I surprised her with a shout of joy!

I am so thankful I was able to go. I will never forget the greeting scene with our new daughter. How overjoyed she was to have a mother, a father, a family. How excited she was about the little things that you and I take for granted: Beds! Showers! Pizza! From the day we met Beth until today she has been a joy to us—filling our own hearts with her overflow. While we were in Thailand we took a trip to the beach, where I took this picture of our new daughter.

But the most amazing confirmation came from a social worker in Thailand. After a few days with our cheerful daughter, I asked, "When my husband and I prayed about adopting Beth, he heard a girl crying. Beth had just had her tenth birthday. What was happening in her life then?" The social worker responded immediately: "She gave up hope. Knowing we rarely find a home for a child over ten, she thought she would never have a mother or a father, and she began to sink into a depression. She was weepy, withdrawn.... But shortly after that we received the news that a home had been found. And her joy returned!"

I do not know why, out of all of the thousands of orphans who need homes, God responded to Beth's cry. I doubt that I will know that until I see Christ face-to-face. But I do know that I would not have had the courage to step out in faith were it not for the wisdom and support my sisters in Christ gave to me.

Our journey with Beth is stretching me, as my friend Sara predicted. Yet as so often happens, my greatest worry has turned out to be nothing. Beth is so skilled that most people forget, after being with her for a while, that she's missing an arm. I do worry that losing her dad after having him for just a little over ten years is too great a blow—yet I also know God is faithful, and I see that, instead of retreating from Him, Beth seems to be pressing in. I also have sisters in Christ who are continuing to pray for her, continuing to love her, and continuing to believe God will complete what He has begun.

This journey through life is filled with danger. As in John Bunyan's *Pilgrim's Progress*, at every turn we may be threatened by bogs of quicksand, lions of ferocity, and the lures of this passing world. How we need sisters in Christ who are truly desirous of living in abandonment to Jesus. How we need to humbly help each other find strength in God.

We Are Sisters!

We belong to an amazing God, and with Him as our Father, we truly are sisters. The blood of Christ is an even stronger bond than the blood of family.

I'd like to close with a prayer for you, my sisters, based on *The Living Bible*'s paraphrase of 1 Peter 3:8.

Father, may we, as Your children, live together like one big happy family, full of sympathy toward each other, and loving one another with tender hearts and humble minds. And may You give us Your blessing as we pray for each other and help each other in any way we can! I ask all this in the power and grace of Your only begotten Son, Jesus Christ.

With much love to you, my forever sisters,

Dee Brestin

SISTERS: WALKING THE ROAD TOGETHER

Reflections

_____

_____

_____

_____

Action Points

_____

_____

_____

_____

NOTES

Chapter 1

1. C. Goodenow and E. L. Gaier, "Best Friends: The Close Reciprocal Friendships of Married and Unmarried Women" (Unpublished paper, 1990).
2. Arlie Russell Hochschild, "Emotion Work, Feeling Rules, and Social Structure," *American Journal of Sociology* 85 (1979): 551–75.
3. Stacey J. Oliker, *Best Friends and Marriage: Exchange Among Women* (Berkeley: University of California Press, 1989).
4. Ibid., 125–26.
5. Anastasia Toufexis, "Coming from a Different Place," *Time*, November 1, 1990, 64–65.

Chapter 2

1. Roy McCloughay, "Basic Stott," *Christianity Today*, January 8, 1996, 26.

Chapter 3

1. Recommended reading from Carolyn Koons, who was a childhood abuse victim by both parents:
   Dennis Linn and Matthew Linn, *Healing Life's Hurts*
   David Seamands, *Healing for Damaged Emotions*

Ruth Carter Stapleton, *The Gift of Inner Healing*

H. Norman Wright, *Making Peace with Your Past*

2. Jennie Dimkoff, "Choosing to Trust," cassette available from 133 W. Maple Street, Fremont, MI 49412.

3. "The American Mother: A Landmark Survey for the 1990s," *Ladies' Home Journal*, May 1990, 136.

4. Lee Ezell, *The Missing Piece* (Toronto: Bantam Books, 1988), 67.

5. Ibid., 69.

6. Gloria Gaither, ed., *What My Parents Did Right* (Nashville: Star Song, 1991), 226.

7. Foster Cline, "Understanding and Treating the Severely Disturbed Child."

8. Gaither, *What My Parents Did Right*, 217.

9. Janice Chaffee, *Sisters* (Nashville: Thomas Nelson, 1995), 11.

Chapter 4

1. Jacqueline Sachs, *Language, Gender, and Sex in Comparative Perspective* (Cambridge: Cambridge University Press, 1987), 178–88.

2. Sydney Taylor, *All-of-a-Kind Family* (Chicago: Follett Publishing Company, 1951), 58.

3. Deborah Tannen, *You Just Don't Understand: Men and Women in Conversation* (New York: William Morrow and Company, 1990), 35.

4. Louisa May Alcott, *Little Women* (New York: Dilithium Press, Ltd., 1987), 3.

5. Moms in Touch International, P.O. Box 1120, Poway, CA 92079-1120 (619-486-4065).

6. Tania Aebi, "Go Away, Little Girl," *Mademoiselle*, April 1990, 227.

Chapter 5

1. Elizabeth Fishel, *Sisters* (New York: Quill, 1979), 39.

2. Ibid.

3. Ann Kiemel Anderson and Jan Reim, *Struggling for Wholeness* (Nashville: Thomas Nelson, 1986), 37.

4. Anne Ortlund as quoted by Jeanne Hendricks in *A Mother's Legacy* (Colorado Springs: NavPress, 1988), 38.

5. Delois Barrett Campbell as quoted by Roxanne Brown in "Sister Love," *Ebony*, September 1989, 29.

6. Laura B. Randolph, "How Sisters Deal with the Fame of Their Sisters," *Ebony*, December 1991, 110, 112.

Chapter 6

1. Stephen P. Bank and Michael D. Kahn, *The Sibling Bond* (New York: Basic Books, 1982), 57.
2. Gary Smalley and John Trent, *The Blessing* (Nashville: Thomas Nelson, 1986), 17.
3. Elizabeth Fishel, *Sisters* (New York: Quill, 1979), 1.
4. Tara Markey as quoted by Dan Morris in "Mom Liked You Best: How Christians Outgrow Sibling Rivalry," *U.S. Catholic*, January 1989, 9.
5. Ann Kiemel Anderson and Jan Reim, *Struggling for Wholeness* (Nashville: Thomas Nelson, 1986), 17.
6. Ibid., 18.
7. Karen Mains, *Don't Give Me That Guilt Trip,* cassette (Wheaton, IL: Chapel of the Air).

Chapter 8

1. Lillian Rubin, *Just Friends* (New York: Harper and Row, 1985), 188.
2. P. O'Connor, "Women's Confidantes Outside Marriage: Shared or Competing Sources of Intimacy?" *American Journal of Sociology* 25 (September 1920): 241–54.
3. Kathie Lee Gifford, *I Can't Believe I Said That!* (New York: Pocket Books, 1992), 272.
4. Elliot Engel, "Of Male Bondage," *Newsweek*, June 21, 1982, 13.
5. Anastasia Toufexis, *Time*, 645.

Chapter 9

1. Ann Cryster, *The Wife-in-Law Trap* (New York: Pocket Star Books, 1990), 2.
2. Ibid., 15–16.
3. Ibid., 145.
4. Glynnis Walker, *Solomon's Children* (New York: Arbor House, 1986), 152.
5. Ibid., 153.
6. Ibid.

7. Lawrence O. Richards, *The Bible Reader's Companion* (Wheaton, IL: Victor, 1991), 42.

8. Cryster, *The Wife-in-Law Trap*, 31.

Chapter 10

1. Paul E. Little, *How to Give Away Your Faith*, cassette (Costa Mesa, CA: OneWay Library, 1973).

2. Crisis Intervention—Keith Hankinson (1-800-504-5280).

Chapter 11

1. Holt International Children's Services, P.O. Box 2880, Eugene, OR 97402.

READERS' GUIDE

*for Personal Reflection or
Group Discussion*

READERS' GUIDE

1. How did Dee's friends engage in "marriage work" in Seattle? Define "marriage work." Have you experienced this either as a recipient or as the one strengthening a marriage? Explain.

2. What do you remember about Dee's friendship with her childhood friend Barbara? Are you still connected to a woman from childhood? What is unique about your friendship?

3. What do you remember about the power of a mother from Lee Ezell's story, Jochebed's story, or from your own life? What, according to the text, are some common responses of women who have been deprived of mother love?

4. What do you remember from Dee's story about mothers who met together to pray for their daughters? List some gray areas that have divided sisters in Christ. What happened to Dee and her friends? What were the keys to victory?

5. What are some of the unique bonds of siblings? Think about your own life as well.

6. What are some difficulties about being the older sister? The younger?

7. One of the keys to overcoming rivalry in our hearts and homes is to be content with how God has blessed us. How has He uniquely blessed you?

8. What do you remember about the triangle? Have you experienced this as a child or an adult? What is God's perspective on this?

9. How might you help your husband, if you are married, understand your need for women friends?

10. Define a wife-in-law and describe her unique challenges. Why is it important and *how* can a wife-in-law live harmoniously with the new wife or ex-wife? What lessons did you learn from Rachel or Leah?

11. What did you learn from Dee's story concerning Amy and Mike? Can you think of a time when a friend helped to restore you to your senses? What did she say or do that helped you?

12. Describe the various ways Dee's "sisters" helped her find strength in God when she was facing a crisis. Have you experienced this personally? If so, share.

13. What two things do you think you will remember from this book a year from now?

Look up Dee on the Web:
www.deebrestin.com
• Write to Dee
• See clips of Dee speaking
• Join Dee's webfriends for inside information
• See Dee's book and movie suggestions
• Purchase books, find sales

The Dee Brestin Series
From Cook Communications Ministries

BOOKS:

The Friendships of Women
The Friendships of Women Devotional Journal
We Are Sisters
We Are Sisters Devotional Journal

BIBLE STUDY GUIDES:

A WOMAN OF LOVE: Using Our Gift for Intimacy (Ruth)
A WOMAN OF FAITH: Overcoming the World's Influences (Esther)
A WOMAN OF CONFIDENCE: Triumphing over Life's Trials (1 Peter)
A WOMAN OF PURPOSE: Walking with the Savior (Luke)
A WOMAN OF WORSHIP: Praying with Power (10 psalms with a
    music CD)
A WOMAN OF HOSPITALITY: Loving the Biblical Approach (Topical)
A WOMAN OF MODERATION: Breaking the Chains of Poor Eating
    Habits (Topical)
A WOMAN OF CONTENTMENT: Insights into Life's Sorrows
    (Ecclesiastes)
A WOMAN OF BEAUTY: Becoming More Like Jesus (1, 2, 3 John)
A WOMAN OF WISDOM: God's Practical Advice for Living (Proverbs)
A WOMAN OF HEALTHY RELATIONSHIPS: Sisters, Mothers,
    Daughters, Friends (Topical)

Dee Brestin offers the perfect companion to *We Are Sisters*

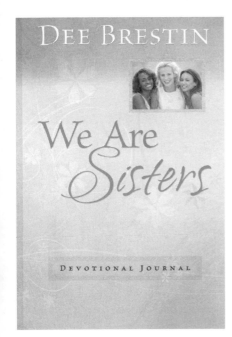

We Are Sisters Devotional Journal
by Dee Brestin

Beloved author and speaker Dee Brestin gave readers a lot to think about in *We Are Sisters*. This sequel to her top-selling *The Friendships of Women* showed women that their special gift for intimacy—coupled with God's friendship pattern—could make their female relationships powerful and nurturing. Filled with a strong biblical focus and personal anecdotes from Dee, the *We Are Sisters Devotional Journal* is the perfect companion in which to record your thoughts and feelings while you explore the unique bonds of intimacy and connectedness that only women can share.

ISBN 0-78144-315-6 • Item #: 104556
Paperback • $12.99

The Word at Work Around the World

A vital part of Cook Communications Ministries is our international outreach, Cook Communications Ministries International (CCMI). Your purchase of this book, and of other books and Christian-growth products from Cook, enables CCMI to provide Bibles and Christian literature to people in more than 150 languages in 65 countries.

Cook Communications Ministries is a not-for-profit, self-supporting organization. Revenues from sales of our books, Bible curricula, and other church and home products not only fund our U.S. ministry, but also fund our CCMI ministry around the world. One hundred percent of donations to CCMI go to our international literature programs.

CCMI reaches out internationally in three ways:

· Our premier International Christian Publishing Institute (ICPI) trains leaders from nationally led publishing houses around the world.

· We provide literature for pastors, evangelists, and Christian workers in their national language.

· We reach people at risk—refugees, AIDS victims, street children, and famine victims—with God's Word.

Word Power, God's Power

Faith Kidz, RiverOak, Honor, Life Journey, Victor, NexGen — every time you purchase a book produced by Cook Communications Ministries, you not only meet a vital personal need in your life or in the life of someone you love, but you're also a part of ministering to José in Colombia, Humberto in Chile, Gousa in India, or Lidiane in Brazil. You help make it possible for a pastor in China, a child in Peru, or a mother in West Africa to enjoy a life-changing book. And because you helped, children and adults around the world are learning God's Word and walking in his ways.

Thank you for your partnership in helping to disciple the world. May God bless you with the power of his Word in your life.

For more information about our international ministries, visit www.ccmi.org.

Additional copies of WE ARE SISTERS
are available wherever good books are sold.

*If you have enjoyed this book,
or if it has had an impact on your life,
we would like to hear from you.*

Please contact us at:

LIFE JOURNEY BOOKS
*Cook Communications Ministries, Dept. 201
4050 Lee Vance View
Colorado Springs, CO 80918*

Or visit our Web site: www.cookministries.com